THE PASSING OF THE EUROPEAN AGE

*A Study of the Transfer of Western
Civilization and Its Renewal in
Other Continents*

BY

ERIC FISCHER

REVISED EDITION

Cambridge, Massachusetts
Harvard University Press
1948

PRINTED AT THE HARVARD UNIVERSITY PRINTING OFFICE
CAMBRIDGE, MASSACHUSETTS, U.S.A.

Preface to the Revised Edition

THIS BOOK was written when World War II was in its initial stages and the Germans as well as the Japanese were still advancing on all fronts. A German victory was still possible, the actual outcome of the war hardly predictable. The author tried at that time to discern trends in the development of Western civilization which would be independent of the outcome of the gigantic conflict. He perceived that Europe's leading position was doomed, whatever this outcome. It was not intended to be a prophecy of the Allied victory. It was meant rather to show that even a German victory could not save European cultural predominance on the globe, not even within the sphere of Western civilization.

Inevitably the emphasis in this second edition has had to be shifted. It is obvious that two essentially non-European powers, the United States of America and the Union of Soviet Socialist Republics, have become politically preponderant. The more is it necessary to stress the development of other non-European nations in South America, South Africa, and Australia as bearers of Western civilization.

There are some changes in the present edition. The essential thesis has not been changed at all, but the reader will understand quite a few pages in a different light under present conditions. It should be kept in mind that this book tells only half the story — the passing of European leadership in almost all ways of life to non-European centers of Western civilization. It hardly touches the problems connected with the renaissance of other civilizations. The ascent of these civilizations to a position threatening European cultural predominance has drawn much more attention from writers than the shift within the nations of European derivation. But a comprehensive study of that development has still to be written. Whether the ascendancy of non-European nations belonging to Western civilization is only a transitional phenomenon or whether they will inherit Europe's global position is hardly amenable to scientific study at the present moment.

Following the suggestion of a reviewer, the original Chapter VIII, "Why Do Civilizations Pass?" has been expanded. Though the purpose of the book is to show trends in present cultural and political development, this chapter is necessary in order to put this phase into accurate perspective by showing the mechanism of the passing of civilizations in general. No biological concept of death is involved. There is every indication that the mechanism of cultural development favors the shift of centers of cultural activity to new locations after a few centuries.

ERIC FISCHER

University of Virginia
May 1948

Contents

Foreword

MOST writers on colonial expansion have been content to discuss the causes of migration from the mother country and the subsequent development of the colonists in their new homes. There they stop. Dr. Fischer, with his thorough knowledge of geography, sociology and population trends, and with his interest in art, architecture and music as well as politics, goes much further.

In his refreshingly new interpretation, he analyzes interestingly the cultural heritage which various migrating peoples took with them and the changes that it underwent in the new homes under new conditions. He then goes a step beyond most other writers and probes the very considerable reflex influence which the new cultural centers later exercised on the mother country from which the emigrants originally came. In the new science of electronics radar measures the impulse sent out from a center and the effect which this impulse has when it bounces back from a distant object to that center. In the same way, Dr. Fischer measures the cultural impulse that went out from the mother country, and then, two or three generations later, the effects which bounced back from the new and distant cultural centers to influence the mother country itself. For instance, the English settlers in America built up a democratic way of life in which Wyoming adopted woman's suffrage in 1869 and was soon followed by many other States of the Union. It seemed to work so well in this country that at the turn of the century many countries of Old Europe began likewise to introduce it. Similarly, American technological inventions and American capital began to exercise a great influence in Europe after World War I.

Dr. Fischer does not limit himself, however, to this reflex action. He rightly sees that there is a continuous reciprocal influence of the old centers upon the new, as well as of the new centers upon the old. He shows how this reciprocal influence has been greatly accelerated by the two World Wars. He might appropriately have entitled his volume, "Civilization at the Center and at the Periphery."

Dr. Fischer is mainly interested in the migrations and cultural interactions of the past century — the expansion of Europeans into America, Africa, Siberia, India, Southeastern Asia and so forth, as well as the earlier settlements of Anglo-Saxons on the Atlantic sea-board and of Spanish and Portuguese in South America. But he also illuminates the more recent shifts of civilizations and their probable significance by parallels with the ancient civilizations which rose and then fell. He compares the effects of the Peloponnesian War and the First World War.

"Passing of Europe" is not quite so pessimistic as the title suggests. Though it is clear, he thinks, that, in general, the Age of Western Civilization is gone, a transformed Western civilization may survive in the new centers outside Europe. In any case, his very thoughtful volume calls attention to the important and unquestioned fact that after this war material leadership and cultural influence will have shifted to a considerable degree from Old Europe to the new worlds beyond the seas and the Urals, especially to North and South America. It is a stimulating book, suggesting pregnant responsibilities, which Americans will find it profitable to read and ponder.

SIDNEY B. FAY

Harvard University

Introduction

PEOPLE living in Europe during the twenties and thirties of the present century felt very keenly that Europe and European civilization could not stand the stress of a second world war. It was a widespread feeling rather than a real understanding of what a renewed, a total, war would mean. People of every country, of every standing, shared this general sentiment. Citizens of the neutral countries such as Sweden and Switzerland shared the feeling with members of the defeated as well as the victorious nations. Some considered such a war inevitable and others thought it improbable, but all agreed that war on a large scale would bring about the destruction of European preponderance in the affairs of the world — even of European civilization. Stanley Baldwin expressed this general feeling when he said, "The very foundation of our . . . Western civilization cannot withstand a second explosion." In speaking so he was the spokesman of people of all classes and nations, sexes and ages. Oswald Spengler's *Decline of the West*[1] was a complicated expression of the same general sentiment in scientific terms. In France Albert Demangeon gave expression to the same feeling in purely economic and far less ambitious, but also less ambiguous, terms.[2]

Meanwhile, there was an undercurrent of unconscious optimism quite as general and perhaps as strong as the sentiment of fear. The great majority of people lived their lives virtually uninfluenced by pessimistic thoughts. This was

[1] Authorized English translation: New York, 1926–28.
[2] *Le Déclin de l'Europe.* (Paris, 1920).

true of those who feared war but considered its coming improbable, and also of the avowed pessimists who professed to see no way to avoid the imminent catastrophe. Only a few drew practical conclusions from their gloomy insight. Some of these became active pacifists, but their number and activity dwindled. They seemed to receive strength rather from the memory of the last war than from dread of the next one. Members of the younger generation who had not experienced the horrors of war were seldom to be found among militant pacifists. And the older generation died out gradually. Some of this older generation forgot or tried to forget the horrors of death and wounds, the dirty boredom of prolonged periods in dangerous, but unheroic trenches, and preferred the role of heroes in the eyes of enthusiastic youth. Even of those who did not forget only a few became pacifists. Others, and these were not very numerous, left Europe driven by the desire to escape the coming imbroglio. Among those who acted on their realization of the approaching catastrophe may be included the silent numbers who refused to have children. The birth-control movement, although primarily fostered by different reasons, certainly drew strength from this source. But most people lived on, practically unaffected, refused to see reality, and seemed to think that somehow, if worst came to worst, they personally would remain untouched.

Such was the attitude of the populations who supported the policy of appeasement. They could not or would not see that it does not suffice for one party to wish to keep the peace; that it may not always be sufficient for both parties to be peacefully inclined, if insoluble questions arise. In spite of their better judgment they believed, because they subconsciously wished to believe. Many Englishmen and

Frenchmen looked away from reality even after the outbreak of war, and did not allow themselves to realize the
cruel fact many months after hostilities had begun.

Such a mass attitude was possible only in the victorious
countries of Western Europe. In Central Europe, including Italy, the tension was too strong for human consciousness and feeling. The signs of imminent danger were too
conspicuous to be overlooked. The psychological result
was that an increasing number of people, especially of young
people, began to consider war essential to progress, avoiding
the dilemma by denying its destructive character. Many
did not deny that war is an evil in itself, but tried to find a
justifying explanation. Of such people the Nazi and Fascist
ideology took hold, with its argument that only the "decadent Western peoples," the bourgeois peoples imbued
with liberal ideas, had to fear a coming war as the end of
their specific, though decadent civilization. Young, powerful, healthy nations would not only survive the coming
struggle but be strengthened by it. German and Italian
youths were taught to see glory in death for the fatherland.
Heroic death on the battlefield would strengthen the moral
vigor of their own country, while unheroic longing for a
peaceful life would lead ultimately to race suicide. Nations
who trembled before the trial of war were declared doomed
and unfit for survival. Consequently, the most extreme
Nazis despised the genuinely peaceful nations — the Swiss,
Dutch and Scandinavians — even more than they did the
French and the English, who in their colonial dominions
had preserved a remainder of the ruling and conquering
spirit.[3]

[3] Christoph Steding, *Das Reich und die Krankheit der europäischen
Kultur* (Hamburg, 1938). Walter Frank, the Reichsleader of the German

There were these three psychological approaches to the problems of the future: the pessimistic, hopeless attitude; the optimistic, complacent attitude; and the optimistic attitude that refused to consider war an essential evil. But they all referred to certain facts as the rational basis for their respective approaches.

The very fact that there are reasons which seem to prove the adequacy of each one of these theories forbids agreement with any one of them. We must formulate a new theory which uses the undeniable facts underlying these three irreconcilable views. The motive for the formulation of our new theory, and hence of this study, is the psychic desire of every healthy human being to find a rational backing for his will to live.

In our opinion, European civilization is shifting its center of gravity to countries outside of Europe. This shift started forty to fifty years ago, and is clearly discernible when we look back from our present situation. For a long time the spread of Europeans and their civilization meant pushing frontiers farther away from a center which became stronger and stronger as it ruled a wider area. Imperceptibly this development has changed its character; the center itself has been dislocated and transferred to other continents, being transformed in the process.

This development is somewhat complicated, since Europe can be called one center only by gross simplification. There were several rival centers in Europe — in Central as well as in Western Europe — and we shall follow their movements as well as that of the general European center.

We shall try to indicate the causes as well as the mechan-

---

historians, wrote an introduction for this posthumous work; the thesis of the book was thereby officially approved.

ism of these historical events. We shall review the different forms of the same process under varying historical circumstances. We shall try to prove that the present disastrous war is only one expression of a crisis in the course of this dislocation and transformation. Since the war, in our opinion, is not a revolutionary interruption of existing trends, but rather the outward sign of a critical turn in those trends, it is possible to a certain degree to indicate the general direction of cultural developments which began some decades ago. A careful review of pre-war trends and a restrained use of historical parallels will help us to find our way.

The Passing of
the European Age

CHAPTER I

Latin America: A New Center in the Making *

THE EXPANSION of Europe beyond her geographic limits began with the colonization of America by the Spaniards. Most of South and Central America is a Spanish-speaking area at the present moment. We shall start our investigation with these Latin-American countries, which have the longest history of all the European settlements.

Despite her older history, South America was outstripped by the United States. Her tempo of development slowed down in colonial times, as the parent countries, Spain and Portugal, were left behind by other European countries. Reactionary governments in Spain and Portugal tried to keep the status of the colonies unchanged. The hot climate may have favored a corresponding inclination among the colonists. But perhaps the most important factor was that immigration to Latin America stopped almost entirely after the first rush in the sixteenth century.[1]

The importance of a cultural center is not necessarily in direct relation to its population, but it is clear that a cultural center can not shift from one continent to another without a movement of population. A few highly influential per-

---

[1] Ernest Gruening, in *Mexico and Its Heritage* (New York and London, 1928), p. 69, estimates that during the whole colonial period not more than 300,000 Spaniards came to Mexico, most of them in the very first decades.

sons — a few missionaries — have sometimes been able to create new cultural centers, but this form of transplantation lies outside the scope of the present essay, since it means widening the sphere of influence without reciprocity. The real *shift* implies a decrease in the importance of the original center, absolute or relative. In consequence it implies that the original population in the developing new center is replaced, or that it is transformed by the influx of people from the old center.

We do not need to know, however, exactly how many Europeans crossed the ocean to Latin America. In most of the Latin-American countries the original pure races are vanishing and being replaced by new mixed nations. As for Spanish America alone, it is impossible to tell how many of its people are of pure Spanish descent, and hardly possible to tell how many are Spanish-speaking. In a number of the Latin-American countries there was no census for many years; in some of them none for more than half a century. The census of 1940 in Peru, for example, was the first since that of 1876.[2] For such a fundamental problem as racial affiliation the official accounts offer rather unsatisfactory and unreliable estimates. Some countries — Chile, Colombia, Mexico — refrain from inquiring into the racial affiliation — a question to which a reliable answer is hardly to be expected.

Take the Chilean example. Most Chileans believe that they are of pure Spanish descent. They point to the fact

[2] For a comprehensive account see Alberto Arca Parró, "Census of Peru, 1940," *Geographical Review*, XXXII (1942), 1. There is no census in Paraguay, Ecuador, or Haiti. In Uruguay, one of the most advanced countries, the census of 1908 remained the only one, in Nicaragua that of 1920, in Bolivia that of 1900. In Costa Rica there was no census from 1892 till 1927, and there has been none since then.

that there are practically no Negroes or mulattoes in the country, and never have been, and that the number of Araucanian Indians is so small as not to alter the predominantly white character of the nation. All this is true. But the immigration from Europe into Chile after the period of the Spanish conquest was small, owing to the remoteness and seclusion of the country, and when the Spanish *conquistadores* came few of them brought their wives; many children sprang from legitimate or illegitimate connections with Araucanian women. These children were baptized and brought up as Spaniards; Spanish settlers who came later intermarried with these first families; after a few decades the influx of immigrants dwindled to an insignificant trickle, and the seclusion of the next three centuries or more produced an even distribution of the Indian strain. It is not very conspicuous, but is strong enough to constitute a particular Chilean type, homogeneous throughout the country and distinctly contrasting with the rest of Spanish South American types. This Indian admixture is so uniform and so evenly distributed that it has become quite unobtrusive, and some observers have claimed that the Chileans were the purest white nation of South America. Undoubtedly the Chileans are physically the strongest and most persevering among the South American peoples, with the possible exception of the Negroes and negro-mixed populations of the tropic lowlands.[3] It is claimed that the distinctive features of the Chilean character are traceable to the miscegenation of a remote ancestry as well as to the scanty and rough nature of the country and climate. Among the original settlers a larger percentage of Basques came to Chile than else-

[3] Charles Edward Chapman, *Republican Hispanic America, a History* (New York, 1937), pp. 4 and 8.

where; and the energetic character of the Araucanians seems to be reflected in the "white" Chileans of today just as the gentle placid nature of the highland Indians is preserved in the character of the Peruvians. Still other observers assert that the Chilean way of soft and swift pronunciation of Spanish words shows the influence of the Indian language.[4] These physiologic and linguistic factors by themselves would have furnished ample basis for provincial peculiarities; but in addition the political development of the country, shut off from the rest of the continent by the Andes, created a historic tradition common to the whole Chilean people and pertinent only to this people. Thus there arose a new nationality.

The process we have described here in some detail for Chile took place in every nation in Spanish America. There are as many different nations in Latin America as there are political units. The borderlines of the original Spanish administrative units left broad zones between the various viceroyalties and captaincies. Most of them were natural boundaries, almost uninhabited — broad strips of desert, virgin forest, or mountain ranges. There have been many conflicts over these empty territories, up to the last war in the Chaco, but the originally settled units are preserved in the republics of today, each with its distinctive characteristics.

In acknowledging the diversity of these nations there should be taken into account the different geographical backgrounds, the peculiar historical traditions, and especially, whether the Spanish settlers were a majority or a

[4] Hubert C. Herring, *Good Neighbors* (New Haven, 1941); John Gunther, *Inside Latin America* (New York, 1941). Gruening, in *Mexico and Its Heritage*, p. 72, mentions as the peculiarity of the Spanish in Mexico the use of many diminutive suffixes — a heritage from the Aztec language.

large or small minority among other races, whether the latter were Negroes or Indians, whether the Indians stood on a low or a high cultural level, and so forth. Only for a few countries is the national character of the later European immigration of any importance; the Italian strain in the Argentinian population is a significant example.[5] Not all these nations have attained the distinction of the Chileans, Argentines, or Mexicans, but all are at least nations in the making.

This is true even for northern Brazil, where the new Portuguese immigrants tend to intermarry with mixed families. The continuous white immigration results not in a strengthening of the white part of the population, but in a lightening of the complexion of the average Brazilian. In Venezuela there are hardly any pure races any more, neither whites, nor Negroes, nor Indians. The last census in Peru gives the number for whites and mestizos (or cholos) under a common heading, although it gives the Indians separately. The number of Indians is still increasing, but their ratio to the whole population is decreasing. Very interesting is the statement that the former craving to be considered a white man is giving way to pride in belonging to the new Peruvian nation.[6] The same change of attitude is apparent in Mexico, where the mestizos are increasing much faster than the pure races, although the Indians are increasing rapidly. Here pride in Aztec ancestors is spreading. Some intellectuals, especially artists, have changed their Spanish names for Indian.[7]

[5] *Encyclopaedia Britannica* (14th ed., 1938), II, 318. Italians in Argentina.

[6] Parró, p. 14.

[7] Gruening, p. 69, contends that in 1805, 18 per cent of the population of Mexico were whites, at the census of 1910 only 7.5 per cent, represent-

Nevertheless, with the exception of Brazil, all these are Spanish nations, connected by the same language and a great deal of common tradition in history, religion, manners, and feeling. There are many very striking similarities among them, especially socially and politically.[8] It is, however, impossible to confine nationality to people of purely or predominantly Spanish descent. The racial and cultural development has rendered it impossible to exclude parts of the population. Hardly ever is doubt expressed as to whether the Spanish-speaking Indians and mestizos of Guatemala or white-red-black mixture of Venezuelans are a nation belonging to the group of Spanish-speaking peoples fully as much as the almost purely white Argentinians or Costa Ricans. Only those Indians who have preserved the purity of their race and still use their own languages can definitely be excluded. It is true that most of the inhabitants of Paraguay speak an Indian language, the Guarani; but the very small ruling minority of whites and mestizos speak Spanish and give to the country its character. There is a revival of Indian languages in Mexico, too. Everywhere else the people using Indian languages are in the minority, and their number, absolutely and relatively, is decreasing. Nobody, however, would deny that both Mexico and Paraguay belong to the Latin-American group of nations. Rather there are some Latin Americans who would like to exclude the Negroes and mulattoes of Santo Domingo. But these very groups were the only ones who ever wanted to be reannexed by Spain, and in this way they gave a practical

---

ing almost the same absolute number. In his opinion about half of these were actually mestizos. The figures for the mestizos were 2,000,000 (38 per cent) and 8,000,000 (53 per cent) respectively; for Indians, 2,500,000 (44 per cent) and 6,000,000 (39 per cent).

[8] Chapman, p. 9.

expression to the feeling of belonging to the Spanish orbit.

Thus, while it is relatively easy to ascertain the percentage of British in the British Isles and outside, it is almost impossible to make an analogous statement concerning the Spanish.[9] The number of Spaniards in America is perhaps equal to that in Spain, perhaps much higher; the number of people who regard themselves as belonging to one of the Spanish-American nations and who use Spanish as their mother tongue is at least double the number of Spaniards in Spain.

The situation in Brazil is similar, except that the European constituent of the population is Portuguese. Therefore it is easier for the foreign student to recognize a distinct nationality in the Brazilians, though in many respects besides language and historical tradition Brazil is much closer to the Spanish-American countries than to Portugal.

During the colonial period Spain paid much less attention to the wishes of her colonies than Britain did. She tried to keep them completely subdued and did not allow even the most insignificant signs of autonomy. Spain herself was governed as an absolute monarchy; the kings had destroyed every local autonomy in the country at the time of Columbus. The Spanish colonists, therefore, had not had the opportunity to learn self-government as the English colonists practiced it. Furthermore, they had not had the opportunity to learn even the daily practice of administration because of the exclusion from officialdom of everyone, even of Spanish family, who was born and lived in America. When

[9] Chapman mentions the official statistics of whites in Peru, Brazil, Mexico and Bolivia, and adds that probably every old family would find some Indian in its ancestry. He even guesses that the ratio of whites to Negroes and mulattoes of Cuba might be reversed if the strict standards of the Southern States of the United States were applied.

the Spanish colonies broke away from the mother country, there were hardly any natives who could handle even the simplest administrative tasks. Many of the internal troubles and difficulties of the Latin-American republics, their generally inadequate government, have been caused by these circumstances — the lack of a working administrative tradition from colonial to independent times. Only in the ecclesiastical administration and in the tradition of law and justice was a break avoided.

During the colonial period Spain restricted the commerce of her American colonies to a few harbors and to her own flag. Under the growing pressure from Great Britain she was not able to uphold her monopoly of overseas trade. Her own economic weakness kept the colonies at a low level and made trade relations with England more alluring. The *asiento* treaty of 1710/11 opened the colonies to English slave dealers, and other merchants, many of them illegally, followed. In 1774 and 1778 reforms inaugurated a new era of better commercial contacts between Spain and her colonies, and a rapid economic growth began, especially in the Argentine colonies. It did not last, however; Spain had no industry, and the period of economic reforms was too short.

Therefore, when the Americas broke away from Spain the disruption was far more complete than the separation of the United States from the United Kingdom had been some years before. As soon as the Revolutionary War was over, the United States and the United Kingdom resumed their traditional trade relations, although not in exactly the same way. For many decades Great Britain remained the main purveyor of industrial products and the main customer for cotton and grain. Despite great disturbances during the first decades, culminating in the War of 1812, the economic

bond between the two countries was strengthened. Moreover, the cultural contact, the natural reliance of the United
States on the old cultural center, was never disrupted. Entirely different from these Anglo-American relations was
the situation in Spanish America after the revolutions. The
economic disruption was radical. The revolutionary wars
had lasted for many years. Spain had been cut off from
commerce by Napoleon's Continental System as well as by
the British blockade. The trade of the Americas was de-
flected completely to Great Britain. Because of the decline
of the Spanish economy after the seventeenth century Spain
was not able to compete with Great Britain, even when the
sea lanes were reopened. Her geographic situation, favorable for the traffic to Latin America, was more than over-
balanced by her lack of modern industry and her general
backwardness. Hence some of the Spanish-American countries became virtually dependencies of Great Britain — dependent on British industry and commerce, but primarily
on British investments. The high-water mark was reached
in the last quarter of the nineteenth century; in later decades
Great Britain had to share her influence with other countries, especially France and Germany. In the twentieth century the United States stepped in, ousting Great Britain
from first place during and through the First World War.
Spain never recovered an adequate share in the economy of
her daughter countries, although Spanish capital and Spanish shipping have recently begun to reassert their interests.

As for Brazil, the rupture from Portugal never was such
a thorough one. The Portuguese royal family fled to Brazil
before the Napoleonic invasion and tried to govern Portugal
from Rio de Janeiro even after the collapse of the Napoleonic empire. The final separation, although caused by a

revolution in Portugal, did not dissolve the political ties completely, because the first emperor of Brazil was the son of the king who returned to Lisbon. Therefore Brazil's liberal empire was in a much higher degree the heir of Portugal than Spain's former colonies were the heirs of Spain's traditions. There was no break in administrative practice, and the standard of the Brazilian civil service in the nineteenth century was above that of any of the Spanish-American countries. This difference in the character of the separation can not be explained merely by the different personalities of the reigning monarchs of Spain and Portugal respectively. A more appropriate explanation is that Portugal was somewhat more liberal towards her colonies than Spain. Another explanation, which should not be overlooked, is that the ratio of the Portuguese population of Brazil to the population of the mother country was much higher than the corresponding ratio in the Spanish-speaking world. The white population of Brazil, at that time almost completely Portuguese, was about as numerous as the population of Portugal itself. Today there live in Brazil about forty million people, most of them using Portuguese as their mother tongue. Even conservative estimates put the number of people of pure Portuguese blood alone higher than the whole population of Portugal. Of still greater consequence, in comparison with Spanish America, is the fact that the whole Portuguese population of the New World is united in one body politic.

Thus it is no mere chance that we find here so early an example of the shifting of the political center of gravity to America. For a decade Portugal was governed from America, although this arrangement was not successful in the long run because Portugal herself was treated as a colony

and not according to her cultural standard, which was certainly not below that of Brazil. The difference in historical
development is the reason why the bonds, both political and
cultural, between Portugal and Brazil were not broken so
thoroughly as those between Spain and her former colonies.

As complete as in administration was the turn away from
the political traditions of Spain. None of the Spanish-
American countries tried to emulate the Spanish monarchy
either in its autocratic form or in its constitution of 1812
and its liberal successors. Republics, however unstable,
arose everywhere. Dictatorships of generals, the so-called
caudillos, superseded the nominally democratic constitutions. These military dictatorships had often very little to
do with military objectives. In many South American countries the army — together with the church — was the only
profession in which the bulk of intellectuals or semi-intel-
lectuals could earn a decent living. Strong personalities,
sometimes ruthless adventurers, used the army to accomplish
their own or their parties' political program. There were
military dictatorships in Spain, too, but the officers in the
Spanish army virtually constituted a political body of their
own, pursuing a separate, purely military ideology. The influential generals in the army were not exponents of civilian
groups, but for the most part represented the idea of military dictatorship in opposition to the ideas of the civilian
political parties. The Spanish and South American military
dictators are hardly comparable.

The most surprising feature in the history of Spanish
America is its radical turn away from the Spanish heritage.
Among the remaining bonds the Roman Catholic Church
was without doubt the strongest. Most of the Spanish-
American countries had periods of anticlericalism, as did

Spain, but such periods were isolated, not even contemporary throughout Spanish America. Besides, the spiritual center of the church was Rome, and the severance of the relations between the episcopal sees in America and Spain was of no great consequence, since the same allegiance bound both to the Holy See in Rome. However, even in countries where the clerical influence remained strong, the nineteenth and twentieth centuries became a predominantly secular period.

Meanwhile, the old and famous universities of Mexico City, San Marco of Lima in Peru, Cordoba in Argentina, still exist as bearers of the Spanish tradition, and they have preserved an unbroken line of tradition until the present day. This is true despite the fact that they have sometimes been the cradle of radical movements in recent times. These universities prepared priests and lawyers, but were at no time the only source of higher education. As early as the eighteenth century, in pre-revolutionary days, Spanish traditions were often superseded by the more fashionable ideas of the French Enlightenment. Some among the higher classes sent their sons to France to be brought up in the atmosphere of the Enlightenment. Although the geographical seclusion, the firm grip of the Catholic Church, and the proud Spanish tradition hindered a swift infiltration of such foreign ideas, they could not be excluded completely, especially since Spain had a French dynasty and her court was open to certain French influences. The government of Spain herself was under the influence of "enlightened" ideas during the second half of the eighteenth century.[10] The victory of French civilization was com-

[10] Arthur P. Whitaker and others, *Latin America and the Enlightenment* (New York and London, 1942), especially the contribution of

pleted when French Romanticism swept over Latin America about 1830. It is true that only a small group could be reached immediately by French literature, but the great masses of illiterate people can not be considered a stronghold of Spanish traditions either. Thus South America culturally became a French dependency, though German, Italian, and British influences were not lacking, the latter especially in Brazil.[11] The literate read their newspapers in both French and Spanish, but never a Spanish book, only French novels and plays. In their business correspondence many merchants used either French or English — the latter because of the overwhelming British economic influence we have mentioned above. Political inclination often followed the economic ties. For example, Argentine was completely dominated by British capital and this circumstance insensibly led to a foreign policy completely in agreement with British policy. The connection was so strong that Argentina came to be called the seventh British dominion. This never was pleasing to the ears of patriotic Argentines; they liked another comparison better and called their capital the Paris of South America.

Despite the foreign influences mentioned, the nineteenth century was for South America a period of almost complete isolation. On the one hand, the severance of its contacts with Spain was very far-reaching, and on the other hand, the connections with France and Great Britain were not strong enough to render it a real outpost of French or British civilization. Native cultural centers were growing slowly, lagging far behind European standards.

Whitaker himself and Roland D. Hussey's "Traces of French Enlightenment in Colonial Hispanic America."

[11] Frederico de Onís, Introduction to *Latin America and the Enlightenment*.

A similar development took place in Cuba when Spanish domination ceased there. The ill-advised Spanish colonial policy had driven the island into open revolt as well as into intellectual opposition. Although a foreign military power, the United States finally accomplished the break: only a few emotional ties to the old country remained. The United States almost immediately assumed the role in economy and politics that Great Britain had played in many South American countries a century earlier. Culturally the United States even rivaled France. New York became for the well-to-do Cubans what Paris was for the people of Buenos Aires or Lima.

Britain's naval actions against Spain and Napoleon had been cited as a proof of her friendship towards the South American republics, but the United States inspired fear in many Latin-American countries by the war against Spain, which seemed only the first step to further conquests. The conflicts of Britain with Venezuela, Honduras, and even with Argentina over the Falkland Islands did not actually harm British influence in Latin America, but by the end of the century the Latin-American republics had advanced so far that they resented an American guardianship.

The appearance of the United States in the Caribbean area made the Latin-American countries conscious of their unity in language and cultural background. Suspicion of the "Colossus of the North" created a movement that favored a more intimate connection among all South and Central Americans. This movement sometimes increased, sometimes slackened, but never entirely disappeared. Some intellectuals tried to find a backing for this movement toward unity — looking toward France, toward Spain, or even toward a united Iberian Peninsula. Some years before the

Spanish-American war a few books had been published de-
nouncing the United States, but the wave of fear and en-
mity against the United States after this war had the effect
of turning many toward Europe for help. The war of Spain
against Chile, Peru, and Bolivia in 1866–67, the French
intervention in Mexico, and the Spanish occupation of
Santo Domingo within the same decade had marked the last
attempts on the part of European powers to rule over
Spanish-American soil. After thirty years of almost complete political isolation, Spanish Americans set out to influence European powers in favor of American political aims.
The semi-colonial period after the colonial period was now
passing. A new center was born that tried to influence the
non-American world.

From the beginning it was no mere political center. The
leading South Americans tried rather to evoke the feeling
that they shared the inheritance of an older and superior
civilization which tied South America to the Latin nations
of Europe, especially to France. Rodó's *Ariel* was the first
attempt in this direction, and it is artistically very valuable.[12] In 1904 a Pan-Iberian Congress was assembled at
Madrid. The number of South Americans in Paris and
Madrid slowly but gradually increased. Even earlier, many
exiled South American politicians had lived in Paris or the
fashionable resorts of Southern France. Some of them had
published books and articles in Paris, but they had not expected their books to be read in Europe. From 1900 on a
slowly increasing number of political refugees chose Spain
as an asylum, the famous Venezuelan writer and poet
Blanco-Fombona, for example. They started to publish

[12] José Enrique Rodó, *Ariel*, translated into English by F. J. Stimson
(Boston and New York, 1922).

their writings in Spain, because they felt or at least hoped that South America was beginning to influence Spain. But it is significant that few South American students went to Spanish universities compared with those going to France or to the United States.[13]

Among the South Americans with Pan-Hispanic leanings, the best known may be Irigoyen,[14] who twice was president of Argentina. The most outstanding political Pan-Hispanic demonstration took place at the Bolivar–Pan-American Congress, held at Panama in 1926.[15] Among other displays of feeling the Mexican delegate proposed to elect King Alfonso XIII of Spain honorary president of the congress.[16] It is doubtful whether this was intended as an anti-American demonstration or as a real expression of growing Pan-Hispanic feeling. In general, the political prestige of Spain was too low, the spiritual bond with France was too strong, for the Pan-Hispanic movement to become important. On the other hand, the Pan-Latin movement, fostered by France, won cultural, but only slight political, importance. It is characteristic that Rodó cites in *Ariel* Greek, French, English, German, a few South American, and even a few American writers — among the latter Emerson, Franklin, etc. — but no Spanish or Portuguese.

Although the Pan-Hispanic and Pan-Latin movements are of less importance than the Pan-American movement, despite its occasional serious setbacks, we must discuss them

[13] Clarence H. Haring, in *South America Looks at the United States* (New York, 1928), p. 173, gives 164 South American students in Spain in 1926, among them 80 Peruvians and 40 Argentines.

[14] Chapman, p. 338.

[15] A hundred years before, in 1826, Bolivar had invited all American republics to a Pan-American congress at Panama.

[16] Haring, p. 119.

more extensively because of their significance for our topic.
Even more significant were the attempts of Spain to use the
Pan-Hispanic movement in her own interest. We have
mentioned that as late as 1867 Spain attempted to resub-
jugate some of her old colonies. Although she had to acknowledge their irrevocable loss, her mental attitude did
not change completely until after the Cuban war. That defeat destroyed Spanish complacency, and although it deeply
wounded the Spanish pride, it evoked a healthy self-criti-
cism. Spanish writers began to recognize the standstill in
Spanish spiritual life, and Spanish intellectuals as well as
politicians began to appreciate the cultural achievements in
America. Though it is certainly not an accurate measure,
the presentation of Nobel prizes gives certain indications.
Spain's Echegaray received the Nobel prize in literature in
1905, but thereafter, for the next thirty years, no Nobel
prize went to anybody using Spanish. In 1936, Carlos S.
Lamas of Argentina received the peace prize, and since
then two other Nobel prizes have been awarded to South
Americans: the prize for literature to Gabriela Mistral of
Chile in 1946 and the prize for science to another Argentinian, Dr. Bernardo Alberto Houssay, in 1947. Spanish
intellectuals had recognized the shift much earlier. They
began to woo the "daughter states." They began to realize
that those states, although politically independent, could
become a source of strength. A century after the loss of the
colonies the idea that "colonials" were an inferior kind
of people died away at last. The Spaniards discovered
that Buenos Aires had become a center of literature
and painting, that some very gifted writers and architects
lived in Lima, and that South Americans had some reason to
call Bogotá the Athens of South America. Still, even in the

twentieth century it was not uncommon for consideration and appreciation to be accorded to outstanding South Americans in other countries, especially in France, earlier than in Spain. The great Mexican mural painters, Diego Rivera — a man of mixed Spanish and Indian parentage — and José Orozco, achieved their fame through recognition in the United States. But Spanish pride was transformed during this period. Instead of boasting of the superiority of the "peninsulares," they began to praise the achievements of Americans as creations of the Spanish genius. The king himself unveiled commemorative tablets in honor of the excellent Nicaraguan poet Rubén Darío and the Venezuelan scientist Francisco José de Caldas.[17] Spain learned that the monopoly of learning was lost, that the center of cultural activity was shifting westwards. The revival of Spanish literature in the twentieth century owes much to the new study of Spanish-American literature. The leftist leanings of many modern Spanish authors can partially be traced to the study of this literature, which often propounded the ideals of the wars of independence.

When the Spanish intellectuals reached this state of mind, they began to visit America and lecture there. They did it without pretending to carry cultural values to less educated peoples, but in an effort to make propaganda for the cultural values of Spain and to convince the South American intellectuals that Spain could offer values as well as France or other countries.[18]

The First World War considerably enhanced the importance of South America, both politically and economi-

[17] Haring, p. 177.
[18] Haring, p. 180, cites the lecture trip of Rafael Altamira of the University of Oviedo in 1909, the first tour of this kind.

cally. In 1899, when the Russian Czar invited most of the countries of the world to the Peace Conference at the Hague, only Mexico among all the Latin-American countries was honored by an invitation. Twenty years later Brazil — and the majority of the small Central American republics — were not only among the original members of the League of Nations, a result of their joining the allied nations, but all the Latin-American nations were invited and most of them accepted. Brazil became a member of the inner council of eight. It is true that two Latin-American countries, Peru and Brazil, had joined the European powers in the race for privileges in China. The Sino-Peruvian treaty was concluded in 1874 in Washington, the Sino-Brazil treaty in Tientsin in 1881. Both belong to the category of the imperialistic "unequal treaties." And that is as far as the alignment of Latin-American countries went. The treaties remained largely dead letters, highlighting the aloofness of the other countries from international affairs.

With the growing impact of Latin America on Europe, Spain's flirtation with these countries became more intense. In 1926 the Spanish flier, Captain Franco, a brother of the present dictator, was the first to cross the South Atlantic from Spain to Brazil and Buenos Aires. Two months later two other Spanish fliers flew to the Philippine Islands to revive there also the pride of the Spanish past. In 1928 an exposition in Seville was devoted to the accomplishments of the Spanish- and Portuguese-speaking peoples. During this whole period Latin-American influence on European politics was never strong, but never vanished completely. It is noticeable, however, that this influence was exerted mostly through the League of Nations, not through Spain.

When the Spanish Civil War broke out, both parties

looked to the Spanish-American nations for moral rather than physical backing. The Franco followers found it in some South American countries, the Loyalists in Mexico. Through Franco's victory Pan-Hispanic ideas became an accepted political program. The phalangist program expounding the twenty-six points of the official declaration stresses the aim to develop a "cultural axis" with Spanish America. The phalange preached "hispanidad," the cultural unity of all nations deriving from Spanish stock, led by Fascist Spain.

But at the very moment when Franco's Spain felt strong enough after her domestic victory to resume an "intellectual reconquest," she again lost the game for leadership. While the phalange made propaganda for intellectual interpenetration, economic coöperation, and diplomatic solidarity,[19] the Latin-American countries, led by Brazil, went over to the democratic side. It may be that the expulsion of so many Spanish scientists, artists, and writers promoted this development. Many of them now teach at universities throughout South America, write in Latin-American newspapers, etc. Since the colonial days, when highly educated churchmen, officers, and aristocratic landowners came over, these refugees were virtually the first to bring Spanish learning and art to the New World and to help in resuscitating old connections; but they also helped shift the center of cultural balance.

Since the days of Columbus, men have left Spain for America; sometimes in great masses, sometimes in a mere trickle. A part of them always returned to Spain, although a small part. During the greater portion of the nineteenth century the emigration was at its lowest level; but during

[19] Haring, p. 168.

the last half century before the outbreak of the Spanish
Civil War about four and a quarter million people left Spain
and only about half that number returned.[20] Almost 80 per
cent of the emigrants went to Spanish America.[21] This flow
of emigrants was not even, but, generally speaking, increased in later years. The emigration from Spain to America may not have contributed much to the tying of intellectual and emotional bonds, since many of the emigrants
belonged to the poorest classes and were often illiterate, but
those countries where the Spanish immigrants constituted
a high percentage of the total immigration seem a bit more
susceptible to the Pan-Hispanic propaganda. Here, however, we can see again a phenomenon already mentioned in
other connections. The influence of the people returning
from America to Spain was somewhat larger, because they
brought a new valuation of the American countries to the
ignorant peasants of the Spanish homeland.

We oversimplify the complicated nature of this shift of
balance if we contemplate the reaction on Spain alone and
not also on other European countries. While the intellectual and artistic center of Spanish civilization is shifting
overseas, while Spain becomes conscious of this fact, the
influence of this new political, economic, and artistic center
is widening. That is the case in Europe, but also in the
United States, where people are beginning to realize that a
new center is arising. Thus Spain is only one of the countries which are of interest for the Latin Americans.

The Pan-Hispanic movement is based on the idea that the

[20] Grover Clark, *The Balance Sheet of Imperialism* (New York, 1936),
p. 48, Table XVIII. According to this table, 4,212,783 emigrants left Spain
between 1886 and 1932, and 2,136,010 returned.
[21] Clark, p. 49, gives 78.9 per cent. Ninety-six per cent of the emigrants
from Portugal migrated to Brazil.

civilization of Spanish America can be intimately related only to Spain, and that political inclination may follow quite naturally. According to this conception, civilization is the equivalent of language. Although this identification of Spanish-American with Spanish civilization is not entirely mistaken, it is not entirely sound either, and is rather misleading. Moreover, political sympathies may sometimes follow economic ties rather than cultural bonds. In shipping and trade, however, Spain had her opportunity just recently. While Great Britain and the United States because of their shortage of tonnage were forced to reduce their services, Spain was in a favorable position, similar to that of the United States during World War I. But she was not able to exploit this opportunity to a considerable degree, and the favorable conditions are rapidly vanishing.

In the present conflict most of the Latin-American countries find themselves opposed to the forces supported by Spain. The latter has not succeeded in influencing them, but rather has been influenced by them. Only later on will it become clear how far Spain was hampered in joining the Axis by her looking towards Spanish America. The impact of Brazil on the Portuguese policy is more evident. There have been rumors at times that an invaded Portugal would entrust her island colonies to Brazil for the duration of the war. Brazil's open siding with the United States destroyed this combination. Here it may be recalled that Brazil was the only belligerent country of South America during the First World War. There is no direct connection, but it is not without significance that in Europe, Portugal, not Spain, joined the Allies.

We know that Brazil often has stood apart from the other Latin-American countries, but at the beginning of this

chapter it was pointed out that the nations of Spanish
America also developed quite distinctive features. One
should, therefore, be careful in citing the Brazilian example
as to the influence of linguistic relationship on political
sympathies. We shall review this influence briefly by considering the general trend of cultural activities.

Latin-American literature, among all the arts, is certainly
the one most open to Spanish influence, since it uses the
common language. In spite of this fact, French influence is
much stronger. Some characteristic national "schools" have
arisen, such as the school of "Gaucho poetry" in Argentina,
the followers of Ricardo Palma's *tradiciones peruanos*,
etc. Some valuable operas have been written in South
America. It is characteristic that the background of the
most valuable musical achievements is both the international
European background and the music of the native Indians.
The Guaranis, an Indian tribe, gave their name to an opera
by Carlos Gomez, and the opera *Ollante* is strongly inspired
by the music of the Peruvian Indians. It is likewise characteristic that these operas were performed, outside of
America, first at Milan and London, not in Spain.

The situation in painting is similar. The achievements of
the Venezuelans are especially well known in France, those
of the Mexicans better in the United States than in Spain.
This fact can not be explained simply by the decline of
Spanish painting, for Spain has painters of first rank in
modern times, such as Zuloaga and Picasso. But the South
American schools have quite distinct national traits; they
are influenced by the painting of foreign countries as modern French painting is influenced by Velasquez, for example. It is pertinent to notice in the paintings of Mexican
artists the square features of their human models and to

remember the similar square features in the stone carvings of Aztec artists in the pre-Columbian epoch. The curved, soft lines of Peruvian symbolic animals are clearly discernible in modern Peruvian arts and crafts.

The best example, however, is offered by the history of architecture, the oldest and most generally practiced of the arts.[22] When the Spanish conquerors had seized the New World, they felt the impulse to celebrate their victories by splendid buildings, churches and palaces. The style of these monuments was, of course, the style of contemporary Spain, Renaissance and later on Baroque.[23] Architects, engineers, artists came from Spain to build these works. Sometimes the plans were drawn in Spain and sent to America to be executed under the supervision of learned monks. But the workers were taken from the native population. In Mexico and the Andean countries there were skilled workmen — masons, carvers in wood or stone, and painters — whose skill was used largely by the Spanish contractors and architects. Almost imperceptibly, and beginning with the external details of the ornamentation, the Indian workmen brought in their own traditional patterns. Geometric carving in Mexico is inherited from pre-Columbian Indian times. Painted patterns on the walls of Franciscan missions in California and New Mexico reveal patterns used in the native pottery of the Pueblo tribes. Although the Spanish masters brought with them a uniform style, the different background of the workers produced variations in the style. The exuberant ornamentation of Aztec buildings is reflected in the rich ornamentation of the Mexican Baroque. On the other hand,

[22] The following discussion is mainly based on the splendid arguments of Talbot F. Hamlin in his *Architecture through the Ages* (New York, 1940), pp. 507–517.
[23] The same is valid for Portugal and Brazil.

buildings in the north of Mexico show the flat, cube-like shape of the pueblos, even in cases where the interior is formed entirely according to the taste of the Baroque. Old palaces and even private mansions in Peru have "great walls of unbroken stone, from which project carved wooden balconies and bay windows like richly ornamented jewels"; they are sometimes rather more like Inca buildings than like buildings in European Spain. Where the Indians lacked an old civilization of their own and had no traditional skill the form tended to be simplified and the details became less elaborate. Cuba retained the closest contact with Spain, not because of its longer-lasting political connection, but because the Spanish had destroyed the original population and were forced to employ white Spanish workers almost exclusively, since the imported Negro slaves could not be used for tasks requiring skill.

Nevertheless, the architecture of Spanish America can never deny its derivation from Spain. The splendid achievements of the very first decades enabled colonial Spaniards to learn from them and to attain the needed practice and qualifications, and it seems that as early as the close of the sixteenth century the architects were mostly colonials. Under the impact of new European developments, new artistic currents arose in Spain, but colonial America had as models for its native architects only the alluring splendor of its own Baroque architecture. Indeed, the Baroque had its own peculiar development here in a period when it was out of date throughout Europe.

At the time of the political severance of Spanish America from Spain, these countries had a style, however intrinsically Spanish, different from the contemporary architectural fashion in Spain, and differentiated throughout the various Spanish-American countries. When these countries severed their ties from Spain, they opened themselves to the impact of all the European styles of the nineteenth and twentieth centuries. The mixture was not always sound, and the architecture of the nineteenth century is not always pleasant.

But the unfavorable conditions of the nineteenth century — political unrest, economic instability, spiritual uneasiness — did not destroy the old traditions. The old churches and buildings still stood, as always, and have influenced modern architects. The countries most advanced artistically clung most strictly to the Latin-American Baroque. In Mexico, for example, this Churrigueresque remained the reigning style almost until the present day. New fashions from Europe, especially from France, may have changed public buildings, but did not change the style of churches and changed only very slightly the living accommodations of the masses, and these only in some big cities. Such buildings were altered in their style only very gradually through long periods, and rather in accordance with changed climatic and social needs than under the influence of foreign styles.

The twentieth century brought some worth-while architectural achievements, the most outstanding being in Peru. There are books concerned with the history of architecture which in their treatment of the twentieth century say more about Spanish America than Spain, and not without good reason. Although it may be too early to recognize any influence of these Spanish-American centers on the older centers, their existence and advanced development justifies the expectation of such an influence. This can not yet be said of all the other expressions of the human mind. But where is the nation which has excelled at the same time in

all respects? The production of philosophical writing may
be of a higher quality in Spain than in Spanish America.
Spain has produced a series of famous novels in the last
decades. One reason perhaps is that while Latin America
has had a tradition in architecture from colonial times, it has
had a native literary tradition virtually only in Peru. Today, however, there are Latin-American writers of the
highest level in the fields of history, sociology, and the
social sciences in general. Despite these developments, however, the slightness of the impact of Latin America on other
countries in all these respects is shown by the fact that modern presentations of Western civilization often skip Latin
America completely.[24]

✝ Spanish America may be a secondary stage in *world*
affairs, it is no longer secondary in the Spanish-speaking
world. We can not foretell whether Spain will recover
from the damages of the Civil War, but her position at the
best will be a bridgehead of Spanish civilization in Europe.
It may be possible, however, that even in this respect English translations of Latin-American authors may open a
much more efficient path of influence. The interest of the
United States in its southern neighbors is growing. Certainly the political point of view is determining this interest,
but interest in cultural values may be roused by the political
movement. Generally speaking, Latin America is becoming
a center of influence — after a period of being an isolated,

---

[24] This is the case in the excellent book of Edward McNall Burns,
Western Civilizations, Their History & Their Culture (New York, 1941),
where only the Mexican painters Orozco and Rivera are mentioned. In
the voluminous work of Harry Elmer Barnes, *The History of Western
Civilization* (New York, 1935), about twenty lines are concerned with
South America. Three painters and five authors are mentioned, who had
influence in Spain or the United States.

neglected outpost, and before that, an object of influences. Isolation was an intermediate status between the colonial state of mind and the self-assertion of the new centers of civilization. When Europe lost sight of Latin America early in the nineteenth century, Latin America was a land of natives ruled by Europeans. Now Europe and North America are beginning to look again toward these countries and to find there a number of independent new nations.

CHAPTER II

From the British Empire to the British Commonwealth of Nations

L ET US TURN to the British Dominions, and see how the center of balance shifted in these countries. It is clear from the outset that we cannot expect to find here an intermediate period of complete isolation such as we found in the history of Latin America. While the uninterrupted political connection did not prevent a period of cultural isolation, it prevented political isolation. This fact puts the political problem in the foreground. The transformation of the political relations between the former colonies and the United Kingdom becomes the leading event, which determines the economic and cultural shift. We shall have to keep in mind the fact that the Dominions have remained within the British Empire. While the impact of Latin America on Europe, however slight, was felt by a number of different countries, we may expect the impact of the Dominions to be concentrated primarily upon the United Kingdom.

The predominance of constitutional problems, which obtrude themselves upon the world through laws, acts of Parliament, and occasionally rebellions or wars, is the reason that the shifting of the center of balance was recognized in the case of the British Empire but nowhere else. It is now generally agreed that the British Empire no longer can be called a European country with outlying dependencies. It has gradually become a non-European, intercontinental power.

For a long time the Dominions were overshadowed by the United States in the Anglo-Saxon world. The English historian, J. R. Green, remarked back in the 'nineties that the future of the English-speaking race would be unrolled on the shores of the Hudson and the Mississippi rather than on the Tweed and the Thames.[1] Conan Doyle wrote from America in 1894: "The center of gravity of race is over here, and we have to readjust ourselves."[2] In 1898, W. T. Stead wrote to Lord Morley: "I feel as if the center of the English-speaking world were shifting westwards . . . "; and in 1901 he published a book under the title *The Americanization of the World, or The Trend of the Twentieth Century*. A Russian newspaper correspondent in London wrote: "Everything proves that Great Britain is now practically dependent upon the United States, and for all international intents and purposes may be considered to be under American protectorate."[3]

But while these authors all paid more attention to America than to the non-European parts of the Empire, they agreed that the center of gravity was shifting away from the British Isles. We believe that they erred in putting the emphasis on America as the *only* heir of Great Britain. There exists an isolated remark by J. R. Seeley showing that

[1] Even earlier there must have been men who predicted such an evolution, for Dilke found it necessary to refute such opinions in 1869. See Charles Dilke, *Greater Britain* (New York, 1869), p. 546.

[2] These and less noteworthy utterances are collected by Richard Heathcote Heindel, *The American Impact on Great Britain* (Philadelphia, 1940), pp. 53, 130, and elsewhere.

[3] *The Americanization of the World, or The Trend of the Twentieth Century* (New York, 1902), p. 14.

this great historian recognized that not only America was influencing Great Britain. He expounded the theory that British history in the eighteenth century was made in America and India and not in England; and he realized that Australasians and Canadians represented new types of men, that the Englishman at home would have to change too; but this remains an isolated observation, and he failed to draw any conclusion.[4] He fought the theory that mature colonies would depart from the mother country as ripe fruits fall from the tree, maintaining that the colonies were a mere extension of the mother country which could remain strictly united to it because of improved means of communication. Most British statesmen of his time, in the middle of the century, considered the overseas settlements destined for independence. So today do non-British observers who try to win the British over to voluntary resignation.[5] In the middle of the nineteenth century these British statesmen did not *desire* the separation, but they looked upon the settlements as children who in due time would establish independent households free from paternal care.[6]

This theoretical recognition of the intercontinental character of the British Empire influenced even political action. The Pan-European plans — the pacifist plan of Couden-

[4] J. R. Seeley, *The Expansion of England* (London, 1883), pp. 10-15.
[5] Characteristic of many is the statement of Nathaniel Peffer ("The Fallacy of Conquest," *Harper's Magazine*, January 1936, reprinted in *International Conciliation*, No. 318, March 1936): "When a colony has reached the stage of development in which it yields the fullest benefit to the ruling country, it has already become economically independent of the ruling country."
[6] Paul Knaplund, *The British Empire, 1815-1939* (New York and London, 1941), p. 202. A. L. Burt, *A Short History of Canada* (Minneapolis, 1942), p. 161.

hove-Kalergi, for example — excluded Britain as well as Russia from Pan-Europe. He considered that both powers were becoming increasingly non-European. The great French statesman Briand, accepting this view, took the first step toward calling this Pan-Europe into existence by summoning a conference of interested countries in Geneva in 1930 from which Great Britain and Russia were excluded. He considered their exclusion from a purely European organization a realistic measure.

Here let it be noted that in stressing the increasingly non-European character of the British Commonwealth of Nations we are concerned only with the British Isles themselves and the Dominions which have a European population. The colonies and India will be touched on later. It is the development of the Dominions that for our present problem is of overwhelming importance.

As the vast expanses of the Dominion of Canada, the Commonwealth of Australia, the Union of South Africa, and New Zealand were filled with European immigrants, a desire for self-government arose. Great Britain had learned from the American Revolution that self-government could not be denied. So she yielded — sometimes very reluctantly, sometimes more generously — to the desire for self-government in her dependencies, especially those populated by Britishers. Thus the claim for self-government became successful gradually, and obtained its constitutional settlement in 1931, when the Statute of Westminster gave legal authority to the statement in the Balfour report of 1926 that the Dominions "are autonomous communities within the British Empire, equal in status, in no way subordinate one to another in any aspect of their domestic or external affairs, though united by a common allegiance to the Crown, and freely associated as members of the British Commonwealth of Nations." [7]

This development of self-government overseas was followed sooner or later by a growing sense of allegiance to the new "Commonwealth of Nations." It is true that the tendencies toward full independence grew also, sometimes in alarming degree. On the other hand, common institutions have developed, based on voluntary coöperation and functioning through mutual agreements.

Three different trends of unequal intensity are clearly distinguishable in the four Dominions. The oldest trend, and for obvious reasons often the only one noticed by foreign observers, is the political tendency to develop self-government to the utmost, to the point where there is only a nominal bond, if any at all, between Dominion and mother country. The Afrikander (nationalist) party of Malan and General Hertzog represent this trend, as does the ruling party in the Irish Free State. A second group of people wish to remain loyal to the British Crown, to coöperate with the British government, but at the same time enjoy self-government without any restriction. They cling to the old loyalty, they cherish a deep-rooted feeling for the old country, they feel that a common tradition, represented by relationship in language and institutions, binds Dominion and mother country together. Sometimes there are material reasons also for this attitude. In each Dominion we find

[7] In this document the expression "British Commonwealth of Nations" is used for the first time as a legal term equivalent to "British Empire." It had been used before, but only as an individually chosen expression — in the title of one of General Jan Smuts' speeches, for instance, delivered on May 15, 1917, and printed in *War Time Speeches* (London, 1917), pp. 17–27. It is also the title of a book by H. Duncan Hall, *The British Commonwealth of Nations* (London, 1920). The expression "the British Commonwealth" without qualifying addition is of course older.

strong parties that are willing to preserve partnership in the Empire but reject any commitment, any responsibility for a common policy. Meanwhile, there is a third group which points out that partnership means commitments, that partnership might assume more favorable shape if the Dominions would not shrink from influencing the common policy constructively. This party is strongest in New Zealand, but is represented also in other Dominions.[8] Moves of the British Government antagonizing the interests of any Dominion are likely to create two different reactions: they strengthen either the desire for full independence or that for shared responsibility. A reaction of the second type resulted in the War Cabinet of 1916, and another, after the British reverses, in the War Cabinet of 1942.

Thus the development of self-government opens two significant prospects. The one is that the British Empire may be dissolved into several independent states, the other that development of self-government, far from leading to a final dissolution, may help to develop a new kind of superstructure, a kind of political organization unprecedented in history, based on the participation of equals — some kind of federal union.

When in 1837 the Canadian colonies revolted, Great Britain was lucky enough to find a clearsighted and brave statesman in Lord Durham. He realized that it was not sufficient to have the power to suppress such a revolution and to carry on with troops, officials sent from the mother country, and the help of some loyal elements in the colony, but that the loyalty of the whole province must be won,

---

[8] A vivid presentation of this point of view concerning the Canadian problem is given by John McCormac, *Canada; America's Problem* (New York, 1940).

and could be won only by the grant of self-government. It is a long way from the first Canadian Parliament, lacking the corresponding institution of a responsible government, to the Statute of Westminster. At present, Britain can be sure of Canadian loyalty without any British soldier or official on Canadian soil, while a century ago a standing army was needed to safeguard the loyalty of a few hundred thousand people there.

It is not necessary to describe the whole development of the Dominions. The present situation is characterized by almost complete self-government. The governors general, though mostly Britishers, are appointed on proposal by the Dominion government. Appeals to the Privy Council are restricted to very few occasions and have been abolished completely in the Union of South Africa for the past several years and more recently (1945) in Canada. The right of the governors general to veto bills has been used only once, in Canada, some years ago. The Parliament of Westminster has retained the right to legislate for the Dominions, but only with the consent of their parliaments — that is to say, practically only in such rare cases as that of Newfoundland. All the Dominions now have diplomatic and consular representatives abroad quite apart from the British Ambassador, Minister, or Consul General. Because of the high costs, and the efficiency of the British service, the number of such posts is not large, but it is characteristic that in the critical period of 1941 Australia set up an embassy of its own in Tokyo. For the first time the right of establishing separate embassies was acknowledged in 1920 — in the case of Canada, the right to send a minister to Washington. But the first minister actually appointed to Washington was an Irish minister in 1923.

There are two remarkable steps in the evolution of the present Dominions from authoritatively governed crown colonies to almost complete statehood. The later one has been mentioned: The Statute of Westminster of December 11, 1931. It somehow closed the period of nascent self-government. It also set the stage for the possible development of the British Commonwealth of Nations, a federation of English-speaking peoples for the most part, whose center of gravity is destined to shift from the European mother country overseas. Such a development has been discussed very often in private circles. Though official policy has not pursued this subject, it was brought into public prominence by a member of the Cabinet a few years ago. Lord Selborne, spokesman for the Government in the House of Lords, has stated that the most effective and democratic development after the war would be to disband the present Parliament, replace it by separate parliaments in England, Scotland, Wales, and North Ireland, and found an Imperial Parliament sitting preferably in a central (!) place like Cape Town.[9]

The other important step, the federation or union of several colonies into one political unit, was reached some time earlier by a few Dominions. Canada in 1867, Australia in 1901, the Union of South Africa in 1910, were constituted by several formerly independent self-governing colonies joining together. It is evident that these new federations and unions were much stronger and better fitted for self-government than the constituent smaller units, although the history of New Zealand shows that this development is not indispensable. Efforts to bring about closer union of the East African colonies are still unsuccessful.

[9] Quoted from the text given by American newspapers of June 1940.

The Dominion of Canada is very much stronger than the single colonies ever could be. The way to expansion and the creation of new autonomous provinces in the prairies was smoothed. The problem of the French Canadians was not solved by the creation of the predominantly French province of Quebec, but it never again became perilous, as it might have been either within a centralist state or in an autonomous self-governing country. In Canada, federation was only one step among others on the route to the present Dominion. In Australia, however, it was the very first step. It is true that the single Australian colonies enjoyed legislative assemblies and even responsible governments. But while the difference between a responsible government in a small territory and in a Dominion of continental extent may be invisible in theory, it is very large in practice. Self-governing colonies may be masters in their own houses, but they are at no time sovereign states and can not have foreign policies of their own. In their domestic policies the Australian colonies were left alone, but they resented it very much that London paid no attention to their wishes when it allowed the French and Germans to occupy Pacific islands which the Australians considered to belong to their zone of influence. It was an exception that "the constant pressure from the colonies finally impelled Great Britain to annex the Fijis in 1874." [9a] This was not repeated as long as the colonies remained isolated. The Australian colonies formed a federal commonwealth in order to be able to influence Imperial policy.[10]

[9a] Werner Levi, *American-Australian Relations* (Minneapolis, 1947), p. 59.
[10] J. Quick and R. R. Garran, *Annotated Constitution of the Australian Commonwealth* (Sydney, 1901), pp. 225-226, do not admit such an interpretation stressing the growing feeling of unity. The pressure from out-

In South Africa two crown colonies, Cape Colony and Natal, existed alongside the two Boer republics. The union of these four heterogeneous territories created a new political unit.[11] The policy of this Union has little in common with the policy of the former British colonies, and it also differs widely from the policy of the other Dominions. Created to reconcile the Boers, the Union came totally under the sway of their political conception, and together with Ireland, took leadership in loosening the ties of Empire.

Australia and New Zealand were more reluctant to loosen the ties, fearing lest such a policy might both weaken the willingness and endanger the moral commitments of the United Kingdom to defend the outer parts of the Empire. Neither of them forgot that their safety from Japanese aggression depended on the power of a mighty British navy. As early as 1921, at the Imperial Conference, the Australian Prime Minister of that time, Mr. Hughes, said emphatically that the Dominions had got all that they could want and that they should not go further; and on August 25, 1937, the Prime Minister of Australia, Mr. Menzies, maintained

---

side — Germans in New Guinea, French in New Caledonia since 1883 — was responsible for a preliminary movement which did not lead directly to the formation of the Commonwealth (p. 110). But most other authors concerned with this problem agree with the statement as given in our text. Even Hall (p. 57) does so, although (p. 86) he quotes Quick and Garran approvingly.

[11] There were trends toward federation in South Africa about the same time as in Canada. They failed, however. More important, though likewise unsuccessful, were the attempts of the Home Government to impose federation. The economically depressed situation of the colonies and the republics in the nineteenth century was the main hindrance to an early solution of this problem. See G. W. de Kiewiet, *British Colonial Policy and the South African Republics, 1848–72* (London–New York–Toronto, 1929), pp. 103 ff.; and by the same author, *The Imperial Factor in South Africa* (Cambridge, 1937).

"that the problem of reconciling independence and unity had not seriously been dealt with so far." [12]   At the Imperial Conference of 1937, Australia and New Zealand barred the move of General Hertzog, then Prime Minister of South Africa, to abolish the status of British subject and to substitute a separate citizenship in each Dominion. Since then, in 1946, Canada has created a separate Canadian citizenship, but without abolishing the British citizenship. There was some talk to the effect that the three Dominions around the Pacific might be better defended if they were to join the United States. Such abstract considerations were overvalued by German propagandists and sometimes by wishful American newspaper correspondents.[13]   Even in the spring of 1942, when the unexpected strength and speed of the Japanese advance induced Australia to look for help to America, both in Australia and New Zealand [14] the basic loyalty to Britain was unshaken. Similar trends were much more real in Canada about 1890 when the commercial ties between the United States and Canada had a tendency to become more intimate, when American farmers from the drought-stricken prairie states flocked over the border, and French-Canadians sought employment in the factories of

[12] Arthur Berriedale Keith, *The Dominions as Sovereign States* (London, 1938), p. 6.

[13] W. T. Stead, *The Americanization of the World*, p. 143, quotes approvingly a Mr. Bakewell, a New Zealand resident, who in a magazine article in 1890 declared that in case of a plebiscite the opponents of a union with the United States would not number as many as one thousand.

[14] Articles by several correspondents in the *Christian Science Monitor* of May 20, 1942, under the common headline: "Whither Australia: Towards the Empire or U. S.?" and C. Hartley Grattan, "The Hope of New Zealand," *Asia*, April 1942. These correspondents had expected that together with the emphasis in both Australia and New Zealand on the community of interest with the United States there would be a loosening of ties with the British Empire. All acknowledge their mistake.

New England and the Middle West, both retaining their original nationality. But there always was a majority of loyalists. English-speaking Canadians incidentally may have fought British "tyranny," but they were always loyal to the "old country" in the depths of their hearts; French Canadians may have disliked the English, but they knew that their nationality could be better preserved in a "British" Canada than among the more than 100,000,000 English-speaking Americans.[15] In general, the attraction of the United States lost strength in the same degree as the ties to the British mother country became invisible and a matter of loyal feeling alone.

This general rule applies even more to the Commonwealth of Australia and to New Zealand. Australia ratified the Statute of Westminster some years later than the other members of the British Empire, and New Zealand has not done so up to the present time.

Such invisible, yet strong, loyal ties to the Empire are hardly to be found in the Irish Free State, and only to a certain degree in the Union of South Africa. Men like Malan and the late General Hertzog and their rather noisy way of expressing their anti-British feelings certainly constitute a real threat to the British Empire, though it should not be overrated. A sober onlooker will keep in mind that in 1905, that is, only three years after the British conquered the Boers, the London government dared to re-institute responsible self-government in the Transvaal and Orange River Colony (Orange Free State). And only five

---

[15] James Bryce, *The American Commonwealth* (1st ed., London, 1888), II, 363, states that the French Canadians living in the United States frequently remain British subjects. This statement was made when the movement for joining the United States was strongest!

years later the Union of South Africa came into existence, a self-governing Dominion, within whose boundaries the original English majority of the Cape and of Natal became a minority. In 1937, the right of the Union to secede from the British Empire was asserted by cabinet ministers [16] and not disavowed in Britain, and today South African troops are fighting side by side with the British. We do not mean to deny the existence of a strong anti-imperial trend, which may become dangerous under certain circumstances. But attentive observers should not overlook the strength of the less noisy, but nevertheless strong, pro-imperial forces.

The Afrikanders, or Dutch-speaking South Africans, do not like to envisage the fact that an independent South Africa would lead a rather precarious existence. The two million whites constituting the "white fringe," though increasing in numbers, would have to face a swiftly increasing number of colored people, at present numbering eight millions.[17] Even General Hertzog admitted that "the white people in South Africa are haunted by a double fear — fear of miscegenation and fear of black domination." [18] But he

[16] On March 30, 1920, Bonar Law said in the House of Commons: "If the self-governing Dominions, Canada, Australia chose tomorrow to say: we will no longer make a part of the British Empire, we would not try to force them. Dominion home rule means the right to decide their own destinies." But it is clear from the debates in the Cape Parliament that this right of secession never was taken for granted.

[17] From 1921 to 1936 the white population increased by almost 32 per cent and the total population (black, colored, and white together) by 38.41 per cent, indicating a still higher factor of increase — namely 40 per cent — for the non-European population. Older census returns pointed to a different result, more favorable to the Europeans. European hygiene and medicine, although granted in small degree, was victorious at last over the unfavorable conditions in compounds, the influence of alcohol, and diseases. (*Statesman's Yearbook*, 1942.)

[18] General Hertzog, in a speech in the Cape Parliament, Feb. 25, 1931, quoted by M. J. Bonn, in *The Crumbling of Empire* (London, 1938), p. 79.

does not admit that the proportion between black and white is becoming much more favorable for the whites, if those two millions are considered the strong outpost of about fifty millions. This fact, however, exists and influences the the policy and position of the Dominion, even if it is not recognized and not admitted. Thus the Union of South Africa is able to carry through an imperialistic policy. It considers itself the natural leader of Africa south of the Sahara desert. An outward sign is the conferences called together by the Union and held on its territory. Thus in 1935 a Pan-African Postal Conference met at Pretoria and was attended by delegates from British, French, Belgian, and Portuguese territories. The next year a Southern African Transportation Conference at Johannesburg was attended by representatives of fifteen territories. The British Empire has to back the imperialistic policy of the Union, willingly or not. Men like General Smuts know this very well.

In speaking of the Dominions we have been concerned almost exclusively with the Dominion of Canada, the Union of South Africa, the Commonwealth of Australia, and New Zealand. It may, therefore, not be superfluous to trace briefly the situation in the two remaining Dominions of the British Commonwealth of Nations: Newfoundland and Ireland.

Newfoundland abandoned her Dominion status under the pressure of financial defaults in 1933, after almost sixty years of self-government.[20] She is now governed like a crown colony, by a governor appointed by the British min-

---

[20] The constitution was granted by Letters Patent in 1876 and was amended in 1905. The first measure of self-government, however, was granted as early as 1853.

istry and advised by a council of six persons, of whom only three are Newfoundlanders. At present a convention is sitting to discuss the future status of Newfoundland, the possibilities being continuation of the commissioner regime, return to Dominion status, federation with Canada, or union with the United States. It is characteristic of the extensive political freedom even under the "autocratic" commissioner regime that such a public discussion is possible, not only in the convention, but also in newspapers and public meetings. As the population amounts only to about a quarter of a million, and the Dominion status is only suspended, not abrogated, as is generally admitted, the whole affair may not seem of much importance in itself, but it may be important in principle. For the United Kingdom did nothing to press Newfoundland to abandon her rights; Newfoundland was forced to this action by her own financial and economic needs. This instance shows clearly that the development from wholly dependent colonies to almost independent states is reversible; [21] forces within a Dominion may arise to recommend a closer connection with the mother country. Similar financial needs made Austria in 1922 accept a financial adviser with very wide powers, appointed by the League of Nations. This acceptance was made easier by the fact that the adviser was a Dutchman. There was much reluctance to yield some part of the sovereignty to the League, but Austria, even in her depressed

[21] After a Negro rebellion, the assembly of Jamaica, stricken by panic, voted for abrogation of the constitution in 1866. In this instance the Home Government only reluctantly accepted full responsibility. Since 1884 Jamaica again has had a working constitution, which is about to be fully democratized by the granting of universal adult suffrage and the reduction of *ex officio* members of the Legislative Council to three by vote of the British Parliament in March 1941.

status, would have absolutely refused an adviser sent by the government of some strong country instead of the League of Nations. The importance of the principle of this transaction within the British Commonwealth is accentuated even more by the fact that Canada, the immediate and intimately interested neighbor, coöperated in adjusting the crown-colony government of 1934.

The commission which advised this temporary solution included representatives of the British, Canadian, and Newfoundland governments. Certainly two hundred years ago, when dependencies and crown colonies as well as territories of a chartered company were considered only from the point of view of the greatest possible gain in income for the mother country, such a commission would not have been trusted. And a country which tries to rule its colonies in order to increase its own prestige, as Germany wanted to do, will not be chosen by a weak country to play the role of an overlord, however temporary. The British Government could be trusted because it had set the example previously of changing from ruler to trustee in its attitude towards its dependencies. Nobody will assume that this change has been completely accomplished — especially in India and in some of the African colonies. There are many governors and lower officials who do not share this point of view, although it has been intimated by the Home Government as desirable. It was perhaps psychologically easier to view white populations or even English-speaking colored people in the Caribbean area under this changed aspect of trusteeship than completely different populations. There have been periods of relapse to former attitudes, but unquestionably a definite start in this direction has been made. Thus the Newfoundland affair, however unimportant in itself, indicates that there is a way to closer coöperation within the Commonwealth of Nations even if it involves abandonment of rights, a way closed almost totally to independent countries by traditional barriers of pride and prestige.

As for Ireland, it must be admitted that Great Britain neglected the role of trustee almost completely. Ireland might have been omitted from this discussion because she is located in Europe. Her geographical location is such, however, that Ireland's connection with the European continent has been almost solely through Great Britain, as with any overseas Dominion. The Irish Free State is only nominally a part of the British Commonwealth of Nations. This is the only instance where the centrifugal tendencies were not balanced by opposing ones in the Dominion itself. The Free State is the only dominion which maintained its neutrality in World War II.

The history of Ireland during the last hundred years offers, besides many diversities, some parallels to the history of the American Revolution. Both countries broke away from Great Britain, because the London government and Parliament insisted on governing them in the interest of the mother country and not in their own interest. But there are significant differences, one of which may be chosen to elucidate further conclusions. "No taxation without representation" is an old English principle. Englishmen living in colonies, therefore, have in general to pay taxes only if self-government is granted to them or if their representatives are admitted to the Parliament at Westminster. This last alternative was never tried in the case of the American colonies, because of the difficulties of slow and sometimes dangerous communication. Most of the American colonies, as well as the West Indian islands, had legislative assemblies

of their own as early as the seventeenth century. A proposed amendment to the Reform Bill, moved by Joseph
Hume in 1831, to give the colonies nineteen representatives
in the House of Commons, failed to obtain a majority. Ireland is the only case where the experiment was tried of en-
franchising a dependency. From the compulsory organization of the Union in 1800 until the creation of the Irish
Free State in 1921, Ireland sent her representatives to Westminster. This establishment was not satisfactory at all to
Ireland, owing to several factors. During the first decades
the bulk of Irishmen were excluded from voting because of
their Roman Catholic faith, and the national divergence was
not mitigated. This is the main difference from the case of
the American colonies, where no national question existed
and an honest consideration of the economic needs of the
colonies might have mitigated most of the resentment. But
the Union was not conceived to give the Irish real influence
in carrying on either their own or common interests. The
British Parliament was to overrule them. Despite these inherent faults, the system worked well for a certain time,
roughly from 1885 to 1914. During this period Irish leaders, notably John Redmond, were prepared to accept the
Union for the time being and to use the British Parliament
for attaining Home Rule. They were able to influence the
British policy, holding a key position between the two great
parties. These Irish leaders had the majority of their fellow
countrymen behind them in pursuing such a policy. But
in general the method of giving representation to outlying
parts of the Empire was discredited by the insincere manner
of its execution in the case of Ireland. Whenever suggested,
it almost unanimously met firm opposition from the Dominions, backed by the many Irish in all of them. People over-

seas were afraid of being a hopeless minority in an Imperial Parliament.[22]   Certainly such an imperial federalism for many of its advocates meant simply reinvigorating the position of the center, England, ruling a unified empire.[23]

Instead of trying to represent their wishes in an Imperial Parliament, the self-governing colonies preferred to strengthen their autonomy, federating themselves in larger Dominions to the same purpose. Finally this augmented power had the same result, enabling the Dominions to influence effectively the policy of Great Britain.

The history of the last few decades offers many examples of the British Government's pursuing a policy dictated by the expressed wishes of the Dominions which would probably not have been pursued if the interests of Great Britain alone had been considered. It is true that the British Government for a long time acted on the principle that it had to take care of the interests of the advanced colonies. In 1904 it conceded colonial rights in West Africa to France in order to ease Newfoundland's burden resulting from old treaties with France. As early as 1871 it conceded to Canadian representatives the right to share the negotiations with the United States because many matters in question were of interest rather to Canada than to the United Kingdom — fishing rights, shipping on the St. Lawrence, and the like. There was no question of putting colonial interests before British interests; Britain acted in the interest of her colonies only in matters which were of no importance to herself and

[22] Hall, *The British Commonwealth of Nations*, esp. pp. 58, 63–67, 222–224.
[23] The most famous spokesman of this group was J. R. Seeley. In his *Expansion of England* (2nd ed.), p. 343, he calls Australians and Canadians "a mere extension of the English race into other lands" and speaks of the colonies as "many Kents."

which she would not have pressed, considering the interests of the United Kingdom alone. In 1899 the British government, press, and public opinion agreed to American plans to fortify Pago Pago, because Australia favored them.[24] Step by step the Home Government was dragged into actions because it did not want to alienate the colonists, though it considered the actions rather contrary to its own interests. In the 'fifties and 'sixties the British Government, being primarily interested in reducing expenses for the colonies, opposed all interference with the affairs of the Boer republics and native tribes beyond their borders. However, "slowly the stream of accounts, of arguments and requests [from the Cape Colony and Natal] was beginning to wear away the resolution of the Home Government," to forbid any annexation of new territory.[25] Many Britons even accused the colonists of starting wars with Maoris and Kaffirs in the knowledge that Britain would finally have to fight them and to pay for them.[26] These less important instances gave way to a series of far-reaching political decisions after the First World War. From that period on it became impossible for the Home Government to formulate a policy without taking heed of the Dominions' attitude. Contrary to its original policy, the British Government asked at Versailles for transfer of some of the German colonies to the British Empire. This "was mainly due to the insistence of the Dominion representatives." [26a] In 1921 Great Britain abandoned her alliance with Japan, yielding to the pressure of Canada, whose Pacific interests were much like those of the Americans. The next year, at the naval conference in

---

[24] Heindel, p. 86.   [25] De Kiewiet, *British Colonial Policy*, p. 207.
[26] See citations from press and Parliament, de Kiewiet, p. 210.
[26a] Lloyd George, *War Memoirs* (London, 1934), IV, 1776.

Washington, Canada induced the British Government to acknowledge naval parity with the United States. Australia and New Zealand induced Great Britain to reassume the fortification of Singapore despite strong opposition by the British Labor Party. The same happened in South Africa. In January 1938 the Union of South Africa declared her readiness to defend Lourenço Marques in Portuguese East African territory. Since a naval force was indispensable for that defense, and since the Union did not possess a navy of its own, this declaration involved the British Government in commitments which it had not ratified beforehand.

The Dominions used the strongest influence in shaping the British policy in the League of Nations. They belonged to the League as original members and were strongly interested in it. In 1920 Albania was admitted to the League by the help of the Union of South Africa and Canada, which overcame the original doubts of Britain. Despite the distinct representation of the Dominions, however, Great Britain sometimes assumed the task of pleading on their behalf. In 1926 the Permanent Mandates Commission asked for more information on British and Dominion policy in the mandated territories. Austen Chamberlain vigorously and effectively protested, although the British Cabinet was not actually opposed to this request, because the Dominions were. The most conspicuous example of the influence of the Dominions was their policy in the Abyssinian war. Many of the then leading British statesmen, among them Sir Samuel Hoare and the Chamberlains, were ready for a policy of appeasement; but the Dominions pressed a policy more in conformity with the principles of collective security.

There is a definite relation between the policy of col-

lective security by international organizations and commitments and the struggle of the Dominions for independence.
For independence involves either suffering an unbearable
burden in defense or securing other safeguards, such as a
strong British navy or a strong League of Nations. However, it seems that the British retreat before the Japanese
aggression in Manchuria in 1931 was largely due to the fear
of a Pacific war expressed by Australia and New Zealand.
And later on the British Government had a strong point in
defending its appeasement policy by hinting at the Dominions' unwillingness to follow Great Britain into a war on
European quarrels. It was even said that the last act of
appeasement, the closing of the Burma Road for supplies to
China during three months in the summer of 1940, was performed by the British Government under Australian pressure.[27]

The general trend is not always so obvious. Sometimes
the Dominions refrained from coöperating in British foreign
policy at all. For example, they did not participate in the
Locarno conference. They officially contended that the
Locarno treaty would bind them to assist Britain in a European war in defense of the guaranteed boundaries, although
they unofficially admitted that it would be almost impossible for them to remain aloof in a war endangering the
existence of Great Britain. This ostrich policy of refraining
from influencing the British policy, of deliberately ignoring
the fact that British commitments were bound to have re-
percussions on the Dominions anyway, was most strongly
criticized in the Dominions themselves.[28] In general, the

[27] Fred Alexander, *Australia and the United States* (Boston, 1941),
p. 25.
[28] McCormac, pp. 71–101.

feeling prevailed in the Dominions that the British Government was the best-fitted instrument to direct an imperial policy because of its relations to all parts of the world and its long experience. A direct influence on the part of the Dominions, it was said, ought to be brought to bear only in cases where this imperial policy neglected the interests of the Dominion concerned. It was thought that if the Dominions exerted their influence too constantly they would become too closely associated with the Empire and would at length impair their full independence. Even after the initial reverses in the Pacific, this attitude prevented the Dominions from participating in an Imperial War Cabinet as they did in the last war. In the First World War this participation was a big success after the disappointment of many circles in the Dominions at being involved in the war without being asked previously. In the last war some people seemed to feel that such participation in an Imperial War Cabinet would necessitate giving up certain rights secured by the Statute of Westminster. After the Japanese onslaught, however, it became clear that a purely British war cabinet, unconsciously overestimating the European problems, would consider all problems from a purely British point of view, and the disadvantages of non-participation seemed weightier than the risk of losing some sovereignty by submitting to an imperial authority. In January 1942, Australia took the initiative in asking the appointment of an Imperial War Cabinet. She recognized that the time had gone when such an imperial authority would be a predominantly British authority. Nevertheless, the appointment of the Australian, R. G. Casey, as State Minister for the Near East remained the only result.

There are a few instances in which the Dominions have

influenced even the domestic policy of Great Britain. As early as 1887 the British Government had ceased interfering with the practice of some self-governing colonies of legalizing the marriage of widowers with sisters of their deceased wives. But until 1906 such marriages were legal only in the colony itself, not in England. In 1907 England adopted the colonial practice in regard to these marriages.[29] In 1914 the United Kingdom yielded to the wishes of the Dominions regarding naturalization of aliens, changing its own legislation so that aliens naturalized in one of the Dominions automatically became British subjects.[30]

More important than such occasional instances when the legislature of the United Kingdom has complied with the Dominions' practice in order to avoid unnecessary complications are those instances when joint committees have been set up to take analogous measures in all parts of the Empire. Characteristically, such examples are generally unknown, because they usually are concerned with a restricted technical field. The names of some of these committees may be sufficient to indicate their fields: Executive Council of Imperial Agricultural Bureaus, Imperial Institute of Entomology, Imperial Mycological Institute, Bureau of Hygiene and Tropical Diseases, Imperial Forestry Institute, Standing Committees on Empire Forestry, Imperial Institute, Overseas Mechanical Transport Council, Empire Timbers Committee. None of these institutes, bureaus, or boards has any administrative or executive power. They do research work, collect information, prepare reports. Even an important

[29] A. Berriedale Keith in his introduction to Gerald E. H. Palmer, *Consultation and Coöperation in the British Commonwealth* (London, 1934), p. xxiii.
[30] Royal Institute of International Affairs, *The British Empire* (London–New York–Toronto, 1939), p. 310.

committee such as the Imperial Defense Committee is a purely advisory body. None of the governments concerned is bound to act according to its advice. But its advice is followed very often. And it can be followed without hesitation for fear of political interference, since the work of all these boards escapes public notice almost entirely, because of its technical or scientific nature. It does not stir up any political preoccupation or suspicion, even when it interferes with practical economic matters as does the work of the Imperial Communications Advisory Commission, the Imperial Shipping Committee, the Imperial Economic Committee, and the Empire Marketing Board.[31]

Some authors [32] have already stressed the importance of these institutions for the coherence of the Empire. Certainly each of them opens a way for forces located in the Dominions to influence the policy of the whole Empire. Through no other channels can this influence work so unrestrictedly. A certain measure adopted in the United Kingdom may have been advocated by an expert from one of the Dominions, or it may be based on experiences overseas, though the general public will not notice it. Conferences on meat supply, copyright, statistics, customs, education, cable and wireless communication, workmen's compensation, the pollution of navigable waters by oil, etc.,[33] are seldom noticed at all, but they can do much to promote unity in manners and style of life and administration. Informal conferences of the High Commissioners who represent the Dominions in London with the Dominions'

[31] The Empire Marketing Board was dissolved in 1933.
[32] Especially Palmer, and Keith, *The Dominions*. Among older authors see Hall, pp. 292–315.
[33] Royal Institute of International Affairs, *The British Empire*, pp. 188–191.

Secretary and a few other members of the Cabinet are very inconspicuous; nevertheless, they are important. They are held without minutes and secretaries, to stress the fact that nobody is obligated by their proceedings. They have become more frequent during the past decade, and it is not impossible to say that their meetings have dealt only with such secondary matters as those mentioned above. Matters of naval defense and the precarious questions arising from the abdication of King Edward VIII were discussed in the same manner.

All these instances mark very distinctly the extent to which the Dominions participate in the government of the Empire. That is why these inconspicuous and informal meetings are of more importance than the Imperial Conferences and the Imperial Economic Conferences. The Imperial Conferences especially mark a step in the development toward autonomy rather than toward shifting of balance within the Empire. In this respect their function is to legalize situations which have developed gradually, and to work out solutions for problems which otherwise might lead to dangerous crises. The whole apparatus of consultation and coöperation described so thoroughly by Keith and Palmers has a meaning for our subject only insofar as it indicates that the direction of the Empire from London alone is a thing of the past. It might theoretically appear that this apparatus could be used to strengthen the influence of a central government in London, but the contrary is nearer the fact.

It is true that this trend to a new integration within the British Commonwealth of Nations was not anticipated when autonomy and self-government were granted. As a general rule, growing autonomy and self-government tend toward separation rather than toward the development just outlined. It is obvious that autonomy of the Philippine Islands, for instance, could not develop in the same direction as Dominion autonomy because of the insignificant proportion of Americans among the Islands' population.

On the other hand the influence of dependencies upon the mother country is not simply proportional to the increase of their white population. Owing to the economic value of colored labor, the position of the Union of South Africa is much stronger than the number of white voters would indicate. Even colonies counting a rather insignificant number of whites — Kenya, Northern and Southern Rhodesia — have accomplished a high degree of self-government, in Southern Rhodesia bordering on Dominion status.[34]

The growth of the white population, however, has been decisive for the increasing influence of the Dominions, together with the increasing speed of traffic and communication, which has enabled them effectively to exert this influence. In 1840 the population of the United Kingdom, which included the whole of Ireland, was about 24 millions, while in the colonies constituting the present Dominions there were only about 2 million whites, the majority of them French-Canadians. Compare with this the present

[34]	*Europeans*	*Non-Europeans*
Northern Rhodesia	18,745 (estimated, Dec. 31, 1943)	1,366,641 mostly Negroes (estimated, Dec. 31, 1940)
Southern Rhodesia	68,954 (census, May, 1941)	1,372,905 Negroes, 6,521 Asiatics and colored (census, May, 1941)
Kenya	**32,054** (estimated, 1944)	3,825,533 Negroes, 61,127 Hindus, 19,012 Arabs (estimated 1944)

situation. Today there are in the United Kingdom — that is, the British Isles without the Irish Free State — almost twice as many inhabitants as there were in 1840.[35] But the white population of the four Dominions, Canada, South Africa, Australia, and New Zealand, in 1938 was estimated to be more than 22 millions (about 11.3, 2.1, 6.9 and 1.7 millions respectively). This population is predominantly of British descent in New Zealand and Australia, and the majority is of British descent in Canada.[36] Thus the white population of these four Dominions now represents more than 30 per cent of the total white population of the United Kingdom and the Dominions together, in contrast to 8 per cent in 1840.

There can be no sure prophecy concerning further developments; but everything points to a continuation of the present tendency.[37] All experts agree that the population of the United Kingdom will no longer increase in any degree

[35] Including North Ireland, 47,175,000, according to an esitmate for June 30, 1946. The census data and estimates for the four great dominions refer to different times. The available data are as follows:

Australia	7,364,841,	census March 31, 1945
Canada	12,119,000,	estimate 1945
South Africa	2,335,460,	whites alone, census August 1946
New Zealand	1,679,972,	census March 31, 1945

That is about 23.5 million whites, compared with a slightly decreased population of the motherland (*Britannica Book of the Year*, 1947; *Statesman's Yearbook*, 1946).

[36] Ninety-eight per cent in New Zealand; 90 per cent in Australia; 52 per cent in Canada, where 28 per cent are French Canadians. In the Union of South Africa more than 39 per cent use the English language; 2½ per cent are bilingual, speaking English and Afrikaans; while almost 56 per cent use the Afrikaans as mother tongue alone.

[37] The best summary of recent population trends is to be found in Frank W. Notestein and others, *The Future Population of Europe and the Soviet Union* (Geneva, League of Nations, 1944). Also valuable is A. M. Carr-Saunders' *World Population* (Oxford, 1936).

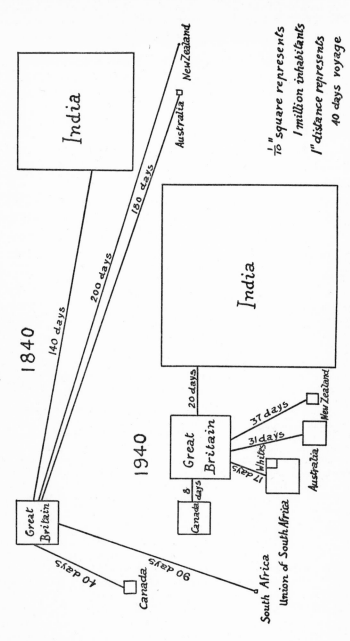

THE GROWTH OF POPULATION AND SHRINKING OF DISTANCES WITHIN THE BRITISH EMPIRE

worth mentioning. Owing to the small size of the age groups which grow up to the marriageable age at the present time, only a tremendous increase of the birth rate could change the trend, and this is rather improbable. There may be some guessing about the exact date at which the actual decrease of population will begin; the expectation of such a decrease sooner or later is general.[38] The size of the population may be affected by other factors also. In the late 'twenties, for example, the British Government favored emigration to the Dominions. But during the 'thirties the immigration and emigration of British nationals to and from the United Kingdom was fairly balanced.[39] It is impossible

[38] Royal Institute of International Affairs, *The British Empire*, p. 305, and Carr-Saunders, p. 128. Exact calculations have been made concerning possible trends in the development of population; see the White Paper on "Current Trend of Population in Great Britain," quoted in Sir William Beveridge's report, *Social Insurance and Allied Services* (London, 1942), p. 91. An older paper shows that in case the level of fertility and mortality rates should remain the same as in 1933, the highest number of inhabitants in England and Wales would be attained in 1943 with about 41 millions and in A. D. 2025 the subsequent decrease would have reduced the number to 22 millions, the equivalent of the present white population in the four Dominions. Should the fertility and mortality rates decline further, then the highest level would have appeared in 1939 and the mark of 22 millions would be reached in 1992. However, the author considers possible a picture — though one of final decrease as well — that shows fertility rates rising again to their 1931 level while mortality remains the same. In this case population would increase to 43.75 millions between 1960 and 1965, and a century later would still be 33.5 millions. The last actual estimate for 1939 seems to justify this point of view. But even so, a decrease is imminent due to the unfavorable grouping of ages. (Enid Charles, *The Effect of Present Trends in Fertility and Mortality upon the Future Population of England and Wales and upon Its Age Composition*, London and Cambridge Economic Service Special Memorandum No. 40, 1935.)

[39] British emigrants in *1938*, to:		Total immigration into the respective countries:
U. S. A.	1,992	67,895
British North America	3,367	17,244
Australia	5,427	9,137

to guess how the present war will affect this development. World War I did not really alter the general trend, though it certainly disturbed the statistical curves in the years of the war itself and immediately afterward. There was a definite increase in the birth rate during the first two years after the war, but it did not last. Nobody can predict whether the present war will cause a more persistent change. It may be that the impact of total war on the whole population will create psychological changes. Much may depend on the situation at the end of the war. One fact stands, however: the death of many young men of marriageable age will be felt — as in every war-stricken country — not only in the immediate decrease of the population through the unusual mortality, but also, and even more, in the reduced number of young married couples and marriages after the war. There is another factor still: thousands of British children have been moved to safety in other countries, away from the dangers of aerial warfare. A certain number of them will never return, but stay with their foster parents.

New Zealand	2,425 (!)	2,386
Union of South Africa	6,003	7,435
India and Ceylon	5,540	....
Other countries	6,390	....
	31,144	

Immigrants of British nationality coming back to Great Britain: 40,611 (Source: *Statesman's Yearbook*, 1942.)

The immediate post-World War II period witnessed two opposing trends: manpower shortages created by the death and the prolonged military service of many young men, coupled with urgent reconstruction needs. On the other hand, a revived desire to emigrate is recognizable, especially to Australia and Canada. This is seriously hampered only by transportation shortages. In this connection, the emigration of war brides to the United States is important, not so much because of absolute numbers, as because the number of prospective mothers in the home country is cut down.

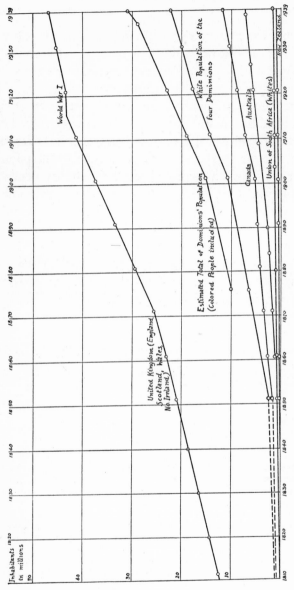

THE GROWTH OF THE POPULATION OF GREAT BRITAIN COMPARED WITH THE POPULATION OF THE DOMINIONS

(The small circles indicate the years of census or estimate.)

This brings the other side of the question into the picture: whether a decreasing population in the United Kingdom, or even a stationary or slightly increasing population, will be faced by an increasing population of English-speaking white people in the Dominions. Even if the number of children now removed from danger zones to other countries and remaining there turns out to be negligible for each particular country, there is still the natural increase — which is quite considerable, at least in Canada and in South Africa. For every 100 women between fifteen and fifty years of age in Canada 132 girls are born who reach the age of maturity.[40] In New Zealand and Australia, for every 100 women in the same age group 98 girls are born and brought up to maturity. But in England the number was only 76, as an average of the years preceding the present war. Considering the English-speaking world as a whole, we find about the same statistics to be true for the United States as for Australia and New Zealand.[41] For South Africa there are no statistics available which can be compared exactly with those above, but from what we can gather we may conclude that conditions are much the same as in Canada.[42]

[40] The numbers are taken from M. J. Bonn, pp. 254–255. The numbers given by Carr-Saunders coincide, but refer to an earlier date.

[41] For a discussion of the American birth rate see *American Journal of Sociology*, July 1942. It can not yet be judged whether today's inflated birthrate in the United States is a temporary postwar matter or whether it will have a more lasting influence.

[42] In 1936 births exceeded deaths by 15.7 per cent among the Europeans in South Africa, compared with 9.7 per cent in Canada in 1940. The average of 1926–30 showed a birth rate 4.3 per cent higher than in 1936, when a rapid decrease took place, although it still remains high enough. Compare this with the excess of births over deaths in 1938 in Australia, 7.8 per cent; in New Zealand, 8.3 per cent (11.9 per cent in 1940); in Scotland, 5.2 per cent (3.4 per cent in 1941); in England and Wales, 3.5 per cent (3 per cent in 1940). The numbers for 1938 here and elsewhere are mostly drawn from *The Statesman's Yearbook*, 1941; the other figures from the 1942 edition.

These statistical computations, it is true, have only limited value regarding the uncertainties of war influences, but the direct losses by the war may be discussed tentatively. Only one dominion, New Zealand, suffered losses comparable to those of Great Britain herself.[43] But there is one factor in favor of New Zealand. The latter may expect some small immigration, while Great Britain is faced with a new wave of emigration.

It is true that migration is still less predictable. Immigration is dependent to a high degree on governmental policy. Immigration policies have changed very often during the last decades, usually in the direction of curtailment. Without any immigration, with demographic conditions dependent on natural increase alone, and discounting the influence of wartime conditions, South Africa's and Canada's population should continue to increase, although their English-speaking sections, as well as the population of New Zealand and Australia, might become stationary after some years.[44] This has been a matter

[43]   WORLD WAR II CASUALTIES

	Killed	Missing	For thousand of population
United Kingdom	244,723	53,039	7
Canada	37,476	1,834	3.5
Australia	23,365	6,030	4
New Zealand	10,333	2,129	7
South Africa	6,840	1,841	3.5
India	24,338	11,754	–
Colonies	6,877	14,208	–
Merchant marine	30,189	5,264	–
for comparison			
U.S.A.	301,000	28,000	2.5

[44] "It is significant that the birth rate in the predominantly French province of Quebec is as high as 25.8 per cent; in British Columbia, which is almost wholly English, as low as 17.7 per cent. In the Union of South Africa from 1931 to 1936 the increase of the European population in the predominantly Dutch Transvaal was 17.9 per cent; in the Cape 5.6 per

of some concern for the respective governments. Only
persons of British descent were encouraged to immigrate
into most of the Dominions, but without conspicuous success.[45] In 1938, the last year of peace, the immigration into
the Dominions on the whole constituted but a small fraction
of the natural increase of their population.[46] Among the
immigrants the percentage of English-speaking persons
varied from more than 50 per cent (Britishers and English-
speaking Americans) into Canada to almost 100 per cent in
New Zealand. This was sufficient to keep or even increase
the percentage of British population in Canada and South
Africa, in spite of their small birth rate, French and Dutch
immigration both being negligible. The prospect that the
English-speaking part of the Canadian population will retain their relative position seems better because of the prospect of Anglicizing, eventually, a rather numerous foreign
population. Of the 20 per cent non-British and non-French-
Canadian population, the major part may become Anglicized in the second or third generation; only a very small
part will be assimilated by the French. The 2.3 per cent of
non-Europeans (Negroes, Indians, Eskimos, Chinese, Japanese) need not be taken into account. The mostly Protestant immigrants from Germany (4.6 per cent), Holland (1.4
per cent), Scandinavia (2.2 per cent) are more likely to be
assimilated by the English than by the French. The immi-

---

cent; and in Natal 6.25 per cent, the last being almost entirely English,
the Cape in its greater part. However, there is a decrease of 2.1 per cent
in the predominantly Dutch Orange Free State, probably owing to local
migration. All these rates exclude African natives as well as Indians.
(Calculated from the figures in the *Statesman's Yearbook*, 1942.)

[45] Cf. second column in note 39.

[46] About 1/6 of the total increase in Canada, Australia, and New Zealand in 1938; almost 1/4 of the increase of the white population in the
Union of South Africa.

grants from Poland (1.4 per cent) and minor groups are mostly settled in the English-speaking western provinces, and therefore are likely to become Anglicized despite their Roman Catholic church affiliations. On the other hand the British emigration, however small, turned more and more to the Dominions instead of to the United States. The average of emigrants from the United Kingdom to the Dominions was only 28 per cent of the total emigration during the decade 1891–1900. It jumped to 63 per cent during 1901–1912, reached the high-water mark in 1912 with 78 per cent,[47] and remained after the war at a considerable height, 55 per cent in 1938 for example. It is impossible to predict the future course of immigration policy in the different Dominions. In any case, immigration is a considerable factor in enlarging the population, a factor not present, or at least not present in such a degree, for the mother country.

There are some other uncertain factors regarding the Dominions. Some observers, for instance, consider it highly improbable that Canada can feed a much greater population in her barren North. Others consider the attraction of the United States strong enough to drain Canada of her surplus for a long time to come. Both Canada and Australia are planning positive steps to further immigration. But opposing trends are unmistakable. Even if the desire to further immigration persists, restrictions on immigrants of British or related descent may endanger the outcome. It would be difficult to estimate the percentage of English and Australian child-bearing age groups lost through war marriages to United States citizens. But it is probable that Australia

[47] L. C. A. Knowles, *The Industrial and Commercial Revolution in Great Britain during the Nineteenth Century* (London and New York, 1921).

won at least as many such war brides as she lost. For Great Britain the final balance is probably less favorable, though we have only partial accounts.[47a]

Summarizing, we see a distinct trend in the development of the population to the end that *the white population of the four big overseas Dominions will become as numerous as the population of Great Britain* sometime during the twentieth century. It is impossible to predict the exact year' or even the decade when this will happen. The war may have delayed, or rather hastened this result, but it did not alter the situation entirely.

Despite all attempts of the governments concerned, immigration has been unable to keep the Dominions predominantly agrarian communities. All the Dominions are rapidly becoming industrialized. They are producing in an increasing degree the same products as the United Kingdom. It is, therefore, impossible to maintain the economic community on a basis of dependency. There must be some partnership which gives influence to the junior partners.

The decisive moment came when Britain agreed to a system of imperial preferences, proposed by Canada at the Conference of Ottawa in 1932. The transition from Free Trade to a tariff with preferences for the Empire was carried through reluctantly under the joint pressure of the

[47a] In the House of Lords the following numbers were mentioned during a debate in May, 1947:

EMIGRATION FROM GREAT BRITAIN

	War brides	Children
to Canada	39,000	19,000
to Australia	3,350	1,100
to New Zealand	2,600	

According to American sources there must be aded at least 25,000 war brides with several hundred children emigrating from Great Britain to the United States.

domestic crisis and the wishes of the Dominions, especially Canada, since 1921. The United Kingdom even pledged itself not to reduce the 10 per cent duty without previous consent of the Dominions. It is true that such a system was proposed by British politicians as early as the time of Joseph Chamberlain, but its final victory was settled, not at the polls in Great Britain, but by the Dominions. "Tariffs themselves appeared an evil thing forced upon the British Nations by circumstances beyond their control, whereas for the Dominion Governments their tariff systems appeared as inherently good, since they were designed to serve national social purposes which had little to do with general arguments about the advantages of freedom of trade." [48]

The few years of peace between the Ottawa Conference and the outbreak of the present war witnessed the difficulties of tying together the parts of the British Commonwealth by means of customs duties. In many respects the Dominions and Britain had become increasingly competitive and no longer supplementary to each other; but it is a fact that the main commercial traffic now flows between the different parts of the Empire more strongly than before. While during the three years preceding the Ottawa Conference the whole Empire supplied only 29 per cent of its exports to Britain, this export began to increase steadily, and reached a pre-war peak of 40 per cent in 1938, the last full year of peace. The Empire received even more of Britain's exports, 43 per cent in 1931 and 49.9 per cent in 1938. As there was a general increase in the trading volume during this decade, the absolute amount is far higher than the percentage indicates, about 50 per cent increase for the exports from Britain to the rest of the Empire and 60 per cent in-

[48] Royal Institute of International Affairs, *The British Empire*, p. 279.

crease for the imports into Britain from the Empire. For a very long time the trade balance has been favorable to the Dominions. While it showed £11,000,000 in 1929 — before the great world depression — it increased to £125,000,000 in 1938.[49] This tendency has continued after the disturbances of World War II. In 1947 for the first time Empire imports and exports exceeded those from and to other countries, in the case of imports even rather considerably.[49a]

These figures are not intended to make a picture of the Dominions gaining at Britain's expense. Indeed, the statistics of the balance of trade and payments show that Britain also gained considerably by this shifting — strengthening her trading position against foreign countries. In emphasizing the influence of the Dominions we are not attempting to draw a complete picture of Britain's commercial relations, but only to prove conclusively that the disintegration of the political empire was accompanied and followed by an integration in the field of economics as well as in spiritual solidarity. This situation has been thoroughly changed by the exhaustion of British assets in foreign countries through the war. But the urgency of exports for Britain is stronger than ever and the dominions are among the few markets open to a certain degree and at the same time capable of

[49] Figures according to Albert Viton, *Great Britain, An Empire in Transition* (New York, 1940).

[49a] UNITED KINGDOM FOREIGN TRADE

Imports	Monthly Average in Million £			
	1938	1945	1946	1947
British countries	31.0	43.6	52.7	58.1
Foreign countries	45.6	48.4	55.4	49.6
Exports				
British countries	19.5	17.8	37.5	42.2
Foreign countries	19.7	15.5	38.5	40.9

Central Statistical Office, *Monthly Digest of Statistics*, No. 18, June, 1947.

paying. The actual flow of trade will crystallize only gradually. It is too early now to predict this accurately.

As for the economic empire, it must be stressed again that the British Commonwealth of Nations is totally different both from the British Empire of the post-Napoleonic period and from the British Empire at the height of Liberalism. The former was a commercial empire, whose outlying posts were for the purpose of serving the well-being of the mother country. The leaders of the latter, the British Empire of the second half of the nineteenth century, recognized the growing disintegration of the body politic and began to wonder whether the remaining assets were equal to the costs of its maintenance. Many of them thought it might be advisable, in the course of time, to liquidate the complex imperial structure, which they considered simply a business venture. Besides, the policy of imperialism from a moral and religious point of view was somewhat distressing to the consciences of men like Gladstone and the humanitarians of the nineteenth century. Even men like Sir Charles Dilke, the most influential advocate of modern imperialism, scorned the worth of "white" dependencies such as Australia and valued highly only the possession of underdeveloped tropical colonies.[50] Despite these adverse currents, the second half of the nineteenth century witnessed a new wave of colonial conquests and acquisitions. Its promoters are discredited today along with their slogans of national virility, national prestige, the white man's burden, the necessity of the flag following the adventurous and pioneering merchant and missionary. Nevertheless, there are still proponents of all these attitudes — the mercantilist,

[50] Charles W. Dilke, *Greater Britain*, at various places, especially at the end of the chapter on Australia.

the liberal-humanitarian,[51] and the imperialist attitude. But the prevailing attitude at present is that which regards the Commonwealth as a partnership, in which the assets should be divided by the partners and will vary in proportion to the degree of coöperation displayed.

In increasing degree Great Britain utilizes officials from the Dominions in the colonial civil service. This may be a first step toward joint administration of the more backward colonies by the more civilized members of the British Commonwealth. Perhaps it is not inappropriate to classify the appointment of the Australian Minister to Washington, R. G. Casey, as Minister of State to the British War Cabinet, with the function of coördinating war efforts in the Near East, in the same category. A partnership not only offers advantages but also presumes joint liabilities, a fact realized more quickly in the mother country than in the Dominions. It seems likely that recognition will come in some Dominions rather in the economic than in the political field. The danger of Japanese aggression taught Australia and New Zealand that they must actively influence the policy of the Empire; economic difficulties seem to have a similar, although delayed, influence on Canada.

Two tendencies have been clearly discernible in the economic policies of countries all over the world for the past decades. One was toward the creation of self-sufficient economic territories with high customs barriers shutting out the world. Representatives of the other tendency, realizing

[51] This interpretation is the underlying idea of Grover Clark's *Balance Sheet*, which tries to reject the policy of imperialism because "colonies do not pay." This materialistic view induced some nineteenth-century English liberals to advocate the voluntary liquidation of the British Empire. This disinterested view incidentally also opened the way for a more human attitude toward the colonial peoples.

the impossibility of complete self-sufficiency, but either unwilling or unable to base the national economy on free trade
and exchange, proposed the federation of smaller units,
either by peaceful agreement or by domination.

Both trends, that toward all-round self-sufficiency and
that toward the creation of larger economic units by federation with other political units, had followers within the
Dominions. The developing industries enforced protective
customs barriers against imports even from the United
Kingdom. On the other hand, the trend toward widening
the economic areas led to the preferential system agreed on
at the Ottawa Conference. Industrial plants grew up in
India and in all the Dominions, especially in Canada. When
a special committee of the International Labor Conference
at Geneva classified all countries according to their industrial capacity, Canada was ranked fifth by one and sixth by
another method of classification. These new industries
often competed with the old established ones in the United
Kingdom. But when the First World War and the world
depression after 1929 closed many factories in England and
Wales and forced others to shift to other products, it became clear that a crisis had been reached: the center of
many industries had shifted overseas and Britain had to accommodate herself to the new situation.

For example: during the First World War the cotton
mills of Lancashire became unable to supply their overseas
customers with the usual wares. New cotton mills sprang
up in India, in and near Bombay, in Canada, and elsewhere.
When the Lancashire mills again tried to serve their old
customers a hard and distressing battle ensued, but the new
competitors could not be dislodged. The 1929 depression
accomplished the defeat of the Lancashire cotton mills and

finally made them turn to other branches of production. In 1938 many of them were working again, using the old buildings and the original invested capital, employing even many of their former workers, but instead of cotton they were producing chemicals.

But the effects of the war must not be overestimated in this connection. Cotton mills were founded in India and elsewhere before World War I. The crisis would have come in any event, though perhaps some years later. It is very doubtful whether a slowly emerging crisis could have been smoothed over. It is not in human nature to accept developments as unavoidable before being forced to do so.

World War II has produced similar effects. The manufacture of airplanes became more and more the special task of the Canadian branch of the joint war industries. Canada learned to make less complicated munitions such as shells during the First World War, but she remained dependent on supplies from Britain in many respects. The fall of France brought a kind of industrial revolution to Canada. Under pressure of emergency British manufacturers sent their secret blueprints and designs to the Dominion. Steel factories, aluminum factories, shipyards arose overnight. In 1942 Canada was scheduled to build as many ships as the British shipyards.

Even more important is the fact that Canada constructed and supplied 95 per cent of the needed materials. As late as 1940 machines and propellers for all ships constructed in Canadian yards had to be imported. This also was very often true of other parts or materials. At the height of the emergency half a million people left the farms for the new industrial centers. Many thousands of unskilled laborers have been trained and are now highly qualified, a few of their instructors having come from the United Kingdom.[52] After the war many factories could be converted. Those people who returned to the farms came mostly from the army, few from the ranks of war workers. Postwar adjustments are not yet completed in the Dominions. But the general result of industrialization already is clearly discernible. It is harder to foresee how the final adjustment in Great Britain will work out. Great Britain is trying to develop her export industries despite all opposing obstacles. Whatever the final success, a new equilibrium will emerge, perhaps in such a way that Great Britain may specialize in certain products. It never again will be the workshop of the Empire.

Other examples might be given: Australia is beginning to construct her own machine tools. She has increased the productive capacity of her textile and clothing industries. A chemical industry, which had not existed before the war, sprang up and came to stay. Also Australian government-owned munitions plants were taken over by private capital and converted to civilian production. South Africa has developed her industries so swiftly that almost the complete equipment of her "Springbok Army" which fought in Ethiopia was made within her borders, from woolen blankets and food preserves to small warships such as minesweepers. An interesting detail is that the armor of the armored cars was made in the Union, but the cars themselves came from another Dominion, from Canada. Australia and New Zealand are more industrialized or at least more urbanized than most of the European countries. Only the

---

[52] This process can be followed in newspapers, and is comprehensively reviewed by Bruce Hutchinson, "Canada's War Effort," in the *National Geographic Magazine*, LXXX, 553–590 (November 1941).

United Kingdom, Belgium, and the Netherlands have a higher percentage of urban population. But all the Dominions have become self-sufficient in many respects during the last two decades.

The general development is manifest. The Dominions definitely have left behind the economic period when they supplied only raw materials and food. Their development into industrialized countries was followed, though reluctantly and only in part, by an adaptation of the British economy to the new conditions.[53] I deliberately use the expression "economy" and not "industry," because there are indications that, for example, Montreal may become an independent financial center on a par with London and New York, a development not initiated but vehemently accelerated by the war. Statistics for 1933 show that in that year Canada borrowed seven and three-quarters billion dollars, but at the same time invested abroad a little above two billion, mostly in the United States.[54] Canadian capital is replacing British capital in the Brazilian power industry.[55] On the other hand, London has been investing its capital more and more in the Dominions, in India, and in non-European countries politically close to the Empire, such as Egypt or Argentina. In 1939 only 7.9 per cent of the British investments abroad were in European countries, and this figure includes Turkey. The war has converted Great Britain into a debtor country. Though its obligations outbalance its still existing assets, the latter were not completely

[53] For two unusually lucid statements on this development, by Australians, see C. Hartley Grattan, *Introducing Australia* (New York, 1942), p. 288.

[54] Royal Institute of International Affairs, *The British Empire*, p. 24.

[55] Lloyd J. Hughlett (editor), *Industrialization of Latin America* (New York, 1946), p. 129.

liquidated and London is still an important money market. Loans were made to Buenos Aires and Moscow as late as 1946. But in order to live, Great Britain strives to export more of its industrial products than before the war. The character of these products is bound to have changed because of the emergence of competing industries in new industrial centers. British industry has to look for markets either for non-competitive products or for other products in the starved markets of Europe. As the relation between Great Britain and the Dominions becomes more and more complicated, it certainly is no longer that of an industrial center to agricultural dependencies. As we consider not only the industrialization of the Dominions, but the adaptation of the British economy to the new condition and a coördination somehow of these two, the resulting impression is a *shifting of the center of economic balance and gravity from the old center in the British Isles to new centers overseas.* Immediately after the outbreak of World War II it became clear to some observers that Britain was becoming economically more dependent on the Empire than the Empire was on Europe.[56]

The shift of balance in intellectual and aesthetic spheres, such as those of science, literature, etc., will be discussed later as part of the European intellectual development as a whole. However, we want to emphasize now the fact that it is the imponderables that prove to be the deciding factors ultimately. All the above-named features are remarkable only in so far as they represent a state of mind ready to make sacrifices for the sake of unity. Reliable observers assert the existence of such a coöperative attitude, still

[56] Troyer J. Anderson, at the meeting of the American Historical Association in Chicago, Dec. 29, 1941.

growing at least in the British segment of the Dominions' population. For this reason some observers expressed doubt whether the enthusiastic welcome given to the royal family on their visit to South Africa in 1947 had real political significance for the non-British South Africans. There is no doubt, on the other hand, that the enthusiasm which greeted King George and Queen Elizabeth on their visit to Canada in 1939 — the first time a reigning king had ever been in one of the Dominions — was a sign of pro-Imperial feeling. The statements of two Australian prime ministers, quoted above, the readiness of the New Zealand parliament to vote a large sum for imperial defense, have to be considered in this view. The growing number of students sent by their parents from the Dominions to English institutions, although the number and quality of the Dominions' educational facilities are swiftly improving, is certainly significant too. Other significant details might be added. Philatelists know that the Australian stamps most in use some time ago had pictures of kangaroos, exotic birds, etc. A recent issue shows the picture of King George VI.

CHAPTER III

"The Americanization of the World"

IN THE PRECEDING CHAPTERS we have seen the difference between the development of the British Dominions and that of Spanish America. Although the Dominions do not constitute a unit, although they are located on three different continents, although their population is far less numerous, and although their civilization is much younger and less distinct, their uninterrupted connection with the mother country enabled them to exert much more influence on Britain than the Latin-American countries did on Spain, Portugal, or Europe generally. Acting through Great Britain the Dominions were even more important for European countries than Spanish America was. This is true if the Dominions are taken as a unit and Spanish America is taken as a unit, and it is true also for every one of the Dominions taken separately in comparison with almost every one of the Spanish-American countries.

Obviously the political factor was the most important in producing this difference of outcome. Other factors may have been responsible too, but it is uncertain how far they were important. There is the difference between Spanish and English background, the existence of a native race in most of the Spanish American countries, the difference in geographical conditions. But the different methods used by Spain and Britain in handling their colonies and the resulting facts of political connection and separation are fundamental.

The United States, as another example in the Western hemisphere, is therefore, especially interesting, since it combines some factors present either in South America or in the British Dominions, and eliminates others. The United States revolted from Great Britain as the Spanish colonies did from Spain, and the political bond was never tied again. The national background of the States, their climatic position, their economic features, resemble those of the British Dominions. We may expect to find the development from an outpost of European civilization to a real nation with its own distinctive civilization following the same line generally; but it is interesting to see to what extent this new nation was able to influence Europe and what other particular features are to be seen in its development.

M. J. Bonn has pointed out [1] that theoretically a partial secondary colonization may go on in the economic, spiritual, and institutional field after the political ties have been broken. We have already emphasized the complete disruption between Spain and Spanish America after the wars of independence. The American Revolution did not have this radical effect. Indeed the American Revolution did not even stop the stream of emigrants from Great Britain to America. Instead, that stream became greater than in colonial times. The result is that there are today more English-speaking people in the United States alone than in the whole British Empire.[2] Considering this migra-

[1] Bonn, *The Crumbling of Empire*, pp. 47, 55, and elsewhere.

[2] H. L. Mencken, *The American Language* (4th ed., New York, 1936), p. 592, estimates that in 1936 about 112,000,000 people in the United States and 62,000,000 in the British Empire spoke English as their mother tongue. It may be noted only as a curiosity, characteristic of the German mentality, that German statisticians often prefer to give the composition of the American people according to the original homeland, in order to offset the impression that there are more English in the world than Germans.

tion as a unit, one feature is remarkable: these British immigrants lost contact with Britain almost completely. Most of
them gave up their status as British subjects and became
American citizens.

It is noteworthy that there are organized groups of
"hyphenated Americans" of most possible kinds, but no
British-Americans, English-Americans, or Scotch-Ameri-
cans.[3] We can call to mind attempts of many of these
groups to influence American public opinion in the interest
of their former homelands (which is not to their discredit —
take for example, the case of relief organizations on a national basis for the starving Greeks today, or for the dis-
tressed Belgians). On the other hand, Americans who make
much of the common Anglo-Saxon background do it as
Americans, not as British-Americans. They are not even
always of British descent. The author of the much-dis-
cussed book *Union Now*, Clarence Streit, bears a non-
English name.[4] These completely Americanized people of
different origins together with the people coming from the
British Isles form the real body of the American nation.

The development of a distinct American nation became

This opens the way for vague estimates. For example, a much-used German reference book, Alois Fischer, *Geographisch-Statistischer Handatlas*
(Wien, 1936), p. 50, puts the number of Americans of British stock at
only 28,500,000 people, and gives the same number for Americans of German descent. He adds some 21,000,000 Celtic Irish. The same author
speaks, however (on page 43 of the edition of 1926) of 76,000,000 English
and Scotch, 8,000,000 Germans, and 6,000,000 Irish. Harry H. Laughlin,
Immigration and Conquest (New York, 1939), using very careful investigations, gives as the proportion of the American people coming from
Great Britain and Ireland 48.95 per cent of the census population of 1920,
4.79 per cent coming from the territory of the present Irish Free State.
  [3] This is true today as it was in the days when James Bryce mentioned
the same peculiarity in his famous book, *The American Commonwealth*
(II, 360).
  [4] Clarence K. Streit, *Union Now* (London and New York, 1939).

evident first in the political field. Economically it was realized much later. The South produced staple products which brought forth a typical colonial economy shattered only by the Civil War. But in the New England colonies an economic type much like European types arose from the beginning. As early as the seventeenth and eighteenth centuries the adherents of the mercantile system looked upon these colonies as the least valuable ones; they drained too much of the manpower of the homeland and produced many things which Great Britain herself could produce. English economists appreciated the products of the forests, which were valuable for shipbuilding, but they tried to hamper the development of competitive industries. Nevertheless, there was always a moderate industry which furnished the groundwork for the rapidly growing industry of the second half of the nineteenth century. But when Europe first began to feel American economic influence it was not from this competitive industry, but rather from the agrarian sector of the American economy. The cotton famine in Lancashire and the European agrarian crisis in the 'nineties, when the Middle West emerged as a furnisher of plentiful and cheap agricultural products, belong to that kind of repercussion which does not indicate the emergence of a new center, but only disturbances due to expanding frontiers. Prior to 1900 two-thirds of American exports were agricultural. Then the ratio changed swiftly, and when the First World War broke out agricultural and industrial products were exported at an almost even ratio. There was a new American economic center comparable to the older European ones.

Much earlier, thanks to the great expositions, the average European appreciated American leadership in technology.

Although the first great exposition in Philadelphia in 1876 exerted only a small influence, beginning in 1887 American products were shown in London almost every year in exhibitions arranged by private initiative. In 1893 the Columbian Exposition in Chicago brought numerous visitors from Europe for the first time. This was perhaps the very first moment when Europeans started to observe American techniques. Staring at skyscrapers and other products of American architecture, they were rather perplexed and did not like them, but they soon learned to study the use of reinforced concrete and steel.

It is a characteristic fact that in American industrial expansion to Europe new inventions and new methods led the way. Almost nowhere were European industries simply taken over and developed to importance; but European products were used until new products could replace them. The steam engine is an English invention; the American Fulton used it for his steamboat. Similarly, Morse made use of European investigations of electricity in his work on the telegraph, an invention which, although of revolutionary import everywhere, was especially adapted to American conditions and needs.

The first American inventions were prompted by the social conditions of a country where enormous expanses with a sparse population needed labor-saving machines urgently. Eli Whitney's cotton gin is a typical example of an invention produced against this social background. It was used chiefly on American soil for many years. Similarly, much later, most of the newly invented American agricultural machines — the reaper, for example — were used only in the United States for a long period. The telegraph had its first extensive use during the Civil War, when military operations had to be coördinated over long distances.

Another early labor-saving machine was the sewing machine (1846). The typewriter (1867–77), the telephone (1875), the electric light (1878), the phonograph (1877), the linotype (1885), and the monotype (1887), all were invented or developed for mass production in America during a few decades. During the 'eighties the number of important American inventions rose rapidly. This development coincided exactly with the opening of an increasing number of branches of American firms in Europe.[5] But the real invasion of the European market took place much later, after the First World War. European manufacturers were forced to accommodate their production to American competition. They did so rather by adopting American methods than by producing products after the American pattern. Before 1929, $60,000,000 worth of American machinery and machine tools were imported annually.[6] German and French manufacturers and engineers used them more intensively than British.[7] Later on, Russian engineers followed suit.

When we mentioned the Columbian Exposition we gave an approximate date for the beginning of this influence. Originally Europeans had considered the tremendous American output possible only at the expense of quality. They

[5] Frank A. Southard, *American Industry in Europe* (Boston and New York, 1931), p. xiii. The first was the Tiffany Company in Paris in 1850; it was followed a short time later by the Pullman Company. Singer & Company opened an office in Glasgow in the 'fifties. From 1880 to 1900, twenty-eight American-owned plants were established in Europe, from 1900 to 1910 almost double that number.

[6] Francis Miller and Helen Hill, *The Giant of the Western World* (New York, 1930), pp. 180–181.

[7] There are plenty of details in Heindel, *The American Impact on Great Britain*, especially in chapter ix, pp. 211–237, but they concern only the United Kingdom.

began to worry about American competition only after the beginning of the twentieth century, and then began to study American technology slowly and with reluctance. It is remarkable that the fear of American competition was much more widespread in Germany [8] than in Britain. In Britain, resentment of American competition in foreign markets, in the Dominions, and lastly in Britain herself, was keenly felt,[9] but it was superseded by the fear of German competition.[10] There were facts which could not be overlooked. In 1900 British suburban railways started to buy American equipment; private individuals began to buy American furniture; commercial offices were supplied with American filing devices; most of the British newspapers were printed with American machinery; American technical processes were reported in the press and followed by a regular public.[11] Despite all this, however, there continued to be a certain disdain for American achievements. The old reputation of European industry persisted even overseas, and together with financial and commercial arrangements it kept American competition from many markets. The South American market was opened to American products only through the temporary elimination of European products during the First World War. That war and the post-war depression in Europe gave American technology and industry a new advantage. Finally, from the middle of the 'twenties, American leadership was no longer questioned

[8] Stead, The Americanization of the World, pp. 169, 179n.

[9] Forty per cent of the American capital invested in European manufactures is invested in Great Britain (Heindel, p. 177).

[10] There was a short scare in Great Britain too. See articles in the press about 1900, and books published at that time, such as, for example, Fred A. McKenzie, American Invaders (New York, 1901).

[11] Heindel, p. 300, states that American technical magazines began to displace the German about 1900.

throughout Europe. German engineers who wished to be considered first-class experts were expected to have visited the United States. Many books on America's industry and technology were published, especially in Germany and France. Rationalization, standardization, serial production, technical division of labor became the characteristic slogans.[12] They all originated in the United States.

This is the general picture. In some particular branches Europeans had acknowledged American leadership much earlier. Those firms such as Singer & Company which used new technical devices were the pioneers. Electrical firms, automobile firms, oil firms are among them. The fact has been mentioned that in some cases American firms not only sold their products, but began to erect their own factories in Europe. In other cases they bought shares in European concerns. The first American industrial investments were made in Europe as early as 1860. In 1929 there were 389 American-owned factories, refineries, and merchandising branches in Great Britain alone. Even after the great depression there remained more than 200.[13]

Thus American capital also began to move across the ocean. Besides the inconspicuous earlier investments, there was a steadily increasing flow which became rather strong between 1900 and 1914.[14] After the First World War, American firms bought shares in European, especially in German, concerns. The technical expression for the economic situation of foreign ownership of plants, shares in

[12] A good description of this period of rationalization so far as it concerned Germany, although the American influence is mentioned only casually, is Robert A. Brady, *The Rationalization Movement in German Industry* (Berkeley, 1933).

[13] Heindel, p. 177.

[14] Southard, introduction and *passim.* M. F. Jolliffe, *The United States a Financial Center 1919–1933* (Cardiff, 1935), p. 7.

companies, etc., is a German word, *Ueberfremdung*, and can be translated only inadequately by "alienation of control." [15] The United States had never known this situation in such a high degree. European, especially British, money had been invested in the United States largely, but rather in state loans, railroads, and banking than in industry.[16] This indebtedness was greatest in the second half of the nineteenth century, but was decreasing steadily. Nevertheless, the United States remained largely the debtor of European countries, primarily of Great Britain, until the First World War.[17] Prior to 1910 there were only three American banking houses with as many as four branches outside the United States, and one house managing sixteen branches, but working only abroad, doing no business in the United States itself.[18] Still, the rise of a new financial center was recognizable. American foreign investment, mostly not in Europe but competing with European investments in Latin America, were five hundred million dollars in 1900. They increased steadily and their amount was about two billion in 1912.[19] At the same time, when these commercial investments started on a higher scale, American loans began to be granted to foreign governments regularly. The great loan for the Mexican government floated by Morgan in 1899

[15] Southard, p. 178.

[16] Heindel, p. 179. Half of the British income from abroad came from the United States in 1899. In 1913 the British had invested in the United States an enormous amount, but it was only a little more than one-third of all their non-European investments, the European investments not taken into account.

[17] Jolliffe (p. 23), besides Great Britain, mentions France, Germany, Holland, Switzerland, Italy, Belgium, Greece, and Japan.

[18] Clyde William Phelps, *The Foreign Expansion of American Banks* (New York, 1927), p. 85.

[19] Henry G. Grady, "The United States in World Trade, an Outline," in *The United States among the Nations* (Berkeley, 1937), p. 38.

was the first of an uninterrupted series of such loans. The
First World War saw the transformation of the United
States from a debtor country into the world's biggest furnisher of capital. From 1913 to 1920 the number of American foreign banking corporations increased from four to
eighty-one. Within the same period the number of American-owned banks and subsidiaries increased from twenty-
two to one hundred, about a fourth of the total being
located in Europe.[20] The amount of American debts abroad
had shrunk considerably. Of the twelve billion dollars —
not counting war loans — lent abroad in 1926, most of the
industrial loans had gone to South America and Canada; but
most of the loans to governments, cities, etc., were placed in
Europe.[21] There is almost no European country which did
not borrow from the United States directly or accept American investments in its industry.[22] The world center of
finance has definitely shifted from London to New York.
Great Britain, indeed, has a larger percentage of its capital
in financial activities with foreign countries, but the total
amount of American capital in foreign business is much
larger.[23] If anything is certain in the continuing postwar
turmoil the trend away from London to New York and to
a few other non-European money-lending centers has persisted, even if it is too early to speak of the liquidation of
the London center.

[20] Phelps, pp. 211–212. These banks were concentrated in five European
countries: Belgium 6, Great Britain 10, France 5, Italy 2, Spain 2. Among
the 61 banks located in Latin America, 26 were in Cuba, 10 in Haiti, and
7 in Santo Domingo. These latter figures represent the situation in 1926.
[21] Barnes, *The History of Western Civilization*, II, 547.
[22] Jolliffe, pp. 104–105. Of non-European countries Canada is the most
important. Argentina, Cuba, Chile, Brazil, Colombia, Japan, and in a
smaller degree Australia and the Dutch East Indies are mentioned.
[23] Jolliffe, Tables XXII–XXIII.

The world depression of 1929 and the following years began with the breakdown in New York, although a secondary center of crisis lay in Central Europe. The American crisis shook the whole world's economy so deeply that in 1931 and 1932 New York was even surpassed slightly in international financial activity by London; [24] but the main trend persisted.

Although the British partner is the most important one in the economic relations of the United States, there can be no doubt that the shift of economic power was a combined result of relations with Europe as a whole. This fact becomes still more impressive if one considers the American economic impact outside of Europe — in the Far East and Latin America. It even seems that the development in these countries was the primary reason for the slogan, "Americanization of the World."

When it was coined half a century ago, this slogan meant by "Americanization" the conversion of the world into a purely materialistic state, where only economic interests and power would prevail. It is characteristic that American tourists in Europe, although often described in fiction and economic literature, have almost never been treated as a factor of cultural influence, but only as a financial asset, or at best, as people who could take European values back to their own country.

This conception of the "Americanization of the World" has been too narrow for some time. It is true that when the slogan was first phrased the shifting had only begun and was evident merely in the economic field. It has become evident since then in other fields, and at the same time for an extended geographic area. In previous chapters we have

[24] Jolliffe, pp. 74, 99.

traced the developing trend in Latin America, we have seen the strong impact of the British Dominions in constitutional matters, we have noted a certain Latin-American influence in the Spanish Civil War. It is no wonder that the strong American economic impact was accompanied and followed by an influence in institutional matters, although it was conspicuously weaker. It might have been still weaker, if it had not sometimes been exerted through the medium of the Dominions.

Certainly the success of the Second Reform Bill of 1867 in Parliament, enlarging the suffrage in Britain, is understandable only against the background of the American Civil War. Still stronger is the American influence regarding women's suffrage. This movement scored its first successes in some of the western states of the United States; Wyoming enfranchised women in 1869, Colorado in 1893, Utah in 1896. The first state east of the Mississippi to do so, Ohio, also adopted women's suffrage before the end of the nineteenth century. About the same time some of the British self-governing colonies followed suit, New Zealand in 1893, South Australia in 1894. The manifest success of this experiment induced the democratic North European countries to enfranchise women in the first years of the twentieth century: Finland first, in 1906; Sweden and Norway a few years later. Most of the European countries did the same in the revolutionary period after the First World War, with Great Britain following very late in 1928.

This is not the only example of America's influence on the Old World acting through the British self-governing colonies. The idea of juvenile courts began in Massachusetts in 1869 and was copied in South Australia before it was adopted in Great Britain. (Here it may be noted that the

colony of New South Wales in Australia, through its enlightened attitude toward crime and punishment, became
the initiator of many valuable and widely accepted reforms
in prison practice. Here for the first time convicts were
sent on leave, and here the method was conceived of meas-
uring the prisoner's behavior through the quality of his
work.) [25] Certainly justice is one of the fields where the ties
between America and Great Britain were stronger than
between these two countries and other European countries.
This was felt when the International Law Association met
for the first time on American soil in 1899.[26] It is, therefore,
the united impact of Anglo-American practice which influenced the European countries. In some matters, however,
the American share was clearly the prevailing one. In European countries juvenile offenders were left unpunished in
former times only if the judges recognized that they were
as yet unable to understand their own actions. In America
the problem of education for juvenile delinquents was
attacked.[27] Furthermore, some of the states of the United
States were the first to try to solve the problem of eliminat-
ing the danger from incorrigible criminals without employing inhuman methods.[28] Americans not only took the first
step but kept on leading in the field of infliction of punishment. As early as 1908 it could be said that Russia, Ruma-
nia, Spain, and Greece were the only European countries
unaffected by American influence in the handling of justice.

[25] Adolf Lenz, *Die Anglo-amerikanische Reformbewegung im Straf-
recht* (Stuttgart, 1908), p. 291. The subtitle, "an essay on its influence
upon the development of law in Continental Europe," indicates the scope
of this book. It comprises all European countries. It is regrettable that
there are no similar special studies for other topics and of a later date.
[26] Heindel, p. 254.
[27] Lenz, p. 260n.
[28] Lenz, pp. 278 ff.

In 1910 the Prison Congress met at Washington. Juvenile reformatories and indeterminate sentences were among the models America had to show the European lawyers and justices. It may be noted that on that occasion a British member of the Congress declared: "This coming of the Old World to the New to learn what lessons the New has to teach is a great historic fact, and may be an epoch in human thought." [29] A second historic fact of probably even wider significance was the conduct of the Nuremberg trials. Justice Jackson's formulation of the principles guiding the court set a mark in international justice. Principles of law and judicial procedure derived from different systems were amalgamated into a working unit. For the first time in history an international court dealt with crimes successfully. And it was done on the basis of principles strongly moulded by non-European, if Western, customs.

We should not grasp the full impact of the American influence if we looked only for those instances in which it actually shaped European institutions. The same is true, though in much smaller degree, for the British Dominions.[30] The American experience was studied, investigated, and quoted, especially in the United Kingdom, on almost every social or political question. In the discussion on the reform of the House of Lords, which dragged on for years, the American Senate was cited again and again, first by the friends of the reform as a valuable model, later more and more as a hindrance to a sound democratic evolution. Like-

[29] Heindel, p. 262.
[30] Cf. such writings as Robert Schachner, "Das australische Sparkassewesen mit für das deutsche und österreichische Sparwesen vorbildlichen Einrichtungen," *Jahrbücher für Nationalökonomie und Statistik*, 89, pp. 65–80 (July 1907).

wise, the American women's suffrage was cited not only by
the British suffragists but also by their adversaries. American experience was used by the Liberals to prove their
points, but as often by the Tories, and sometimes by the
Laborites. Sometimes opposing parties both cited the
American example.[32]

This impact of the American pattern was to be seen in
other European countries too, although it was much weaker
and only intermittent. Lafayette and other Frenchmen who
had fought in America took back to France the republican
ideals, the idea of the rights of man, etc. After a few years
this influence came to an end, because no new provocative
ideas followed. Then, too, the influence of Tocqueville's
famous book [33] on the European and especially on the
French theory of Liberalism remained only one isolated
fact. But a study of the different constitutions created by
the new European states after 1918 shows that in large
measure the American pattern had superseded the pattern
of the nineteenth century, British parliamentarism and the
French and Belgian constitutions. It had come to have at
least an equal influence. But again we can see that in the
British Dominions this institutional influence started much
earlier. The Canadian federal constitution of 1867 and the
Australian constitution of 1901 owe much to the American
pattern. Such acceptance was much easier where no questions of American power seemed involved. The draft of the
constitution for the League of Nations was accepted by
many European governments only reluctantly, but supreme
courts, formed according to the American pattern, were
created in many countries, and the definition of presidential

[32] Heindel cites such controversies often and extensively, especially in
the second half of his book.
[33] Alexis de Tocqueville, *De la démocratie en Amérique* (1835).

competence and the formation of a states chamber in the Austrian constitution were based on American thought and experience.

It is, accordingly, possible to trace American influence on European domestic developments. Of course this influence was strongest and most continuous in Britain. We may venture to assert that from the end of the nineteenth century Britain began to give serious consideration to public opinion in the United States. The last time British public opinion paid too little attention to American public opinion was during the Venezuelan border dispute. Confronted with the unexpected danger of war, Britain shrank back.[34] Later, Britain followed her course in the Boer War undisturbed by the vociferous disapproval of public opinion in Europe, but was very anxious to win American public opinion for her cause. Generally speaking, the *New York Times* does not influence British policy as does the London *Times*, but it is only a difference in degree.

It is significant that the first full-time English newspaper correspondent residing in the United States was not appointed until 1910. Since then American newspapers have spread in Europe, especially in Britain. From 1914 to the outbreak of the present war they have trebled their number of subscribers.

British readiness to hear the expression of American public opinion becomes manifest in the Irish question. The influence of the Irish in America on their brethren in Eire has always been strong. They have offered a home to masses of emigrants;[35] they have sent money to poverty-stricken

---

[34] N. M. Blake, "Background of Cleveland's Venezuelan Policy," *American Historical Review*, XLVII, 259–278 (January 1942).

[35] Between 1845 and 1865 about 1,500,000 persons left Ireland for America.

relatives in Eire; they started the movement for the revival of the old national Gaelic language; they formed revolutionary societies on American soil which furnished propaganda, money, bombs, and guns for the struggle in Ireland.[36] The demobilized soldiers of the American Civil War organized the first bands of Fenians [37] who tried to invade Canada and to fight for Eire's freedom on Canadian soil. These failed; but the concessions of 1867 were wrung by them from the British. Parnell's policy in the late 'seventies and early 'eighties was dictated partly by regard for Clan-na-Gael, the American Fenian organization. Parnell kept his own line of policy, but the thousands of pamphlets inciting to assassinations did their work also. The Fenians saw their main hope in a coming war between Great Britain and the United States; but they never succeeded in pushing American opinion in this direction.

The bulk of the Irish were poor, uneducated, separated from the majority of the Americans by their Roman Catholic faith. Nevertheless, their increasing number and their political shrewdness forced the political parties, as well as public opinion, to pay attention to their grievances. The number of Irishmen in the newspaper profession as owners, shareholders, and journalists, as well as in local politics, was an important factor. It may remain doubtful whether hostility toward Britain on the part of the Irish-Americans actually retarded America's entry into the First and Second

[36] Tom Ireland, *Ireland; Past and Present* (New York, 1941), refers again and again to instances when the British policy was shaped by regard for America. Other histories of Ireland could be consulted likewise. Tom Ireland's is the latest and gives many details.

[37] The Fenian brotherhood was founded by John O'Mahoney in 1858 with the express purpose of attaining complete political independence for Ireland by force of arms.

World Wars;[38] it is less doubtful that America helped to convince the British statesmen that they could not evade the creation of the Irish Free State. American help went so far as to tolerate the raising of funds for the Irish rebels in open defiance of American criminal law. It is rather doubtful whether such open collections for rebels of any other nation would have been tolerated.[39]

It may be noted that Irish influence is a not at all negligible factor in the relations between Great Britain and the Dominions. An Australian observer remarked:[39a] "A never negligible body of feeling rather than of reasoned opinion was always influenced by the aim of assisting political movements in Ireland."

The Irish case is perhaps the only instance where American interference in behalf of a particular European nation has been prompted by its former nationals who have become citizens of the United States. The interference of the United States in behalf of the cruelly suppressed Armenians can not be traced to the very few Armenians living in the United States, and the entrance of America into the Second World War must be traced much more to common interest in the maintenance of democratic ideas and the primitive fact that a first-rate power can not remain unaffected by a world-wide conflict than to agitation on the part of any national group, although it can not be denied that the Anglo-Saxon tradition contributed in a minor degree to this war decision.

These latter points have led us imperceptibly from the field of institutions and public opinion to foreign policy.

[38] So Ireland, p. 41. Other authors mention this influence, though less positively.

[39] Ireland, p. 363.

[39a] A. Greenfell Price, *Australia Comes of Age* (Melbourne, 1945).

Three times during the last three decades America has stepped into European affairs. Her entry into the First World War decided its outcome. The Covenant of the League of Nations was forced upon rather unwilling European governments and more ready peoples by Wilson though he was backed by only a part of American public opinion. Likewise the entry of the United States into World War II decided the final outcome. But America was afraid of entanglements as were the British Dominions, and refrained from exerting an influence which was almost pressed upon her. It is evident that America had an active political influence even during the years when she pursued a policy of isolation and tried to avoid all European entanglements. She never could hinder American loans from being sought and given, and Americans from becoming interested in the stability of certain regimes to which money had been loaned. And these borrowing governments became stronger by the financial backing they had obtained from America.[40] (Here it may be observed that although America tried to keep out of European affairs, the same can not be said for the Far East, and, since the Spanish American War, for the Caribbean area.)

In general we may say that the break from Great Britain slowed down the growth of the political and institutional influence of the United States, or postponed it in several respects for many decades. The break, however, offered the advantage of an unhampered and swifter growth of a strong independent economy. Probably, for example, the influx of immigrants into a dependent America from other European countries would have been much slower. Would

[40] It is perhaps too early to estimate the real influence of American loans in stabilizing such regimes as Pilsudski's, Mussolini's, and Franco's.

a British America have been the desired country for the Irish, for the political refugees from Germany in the wake of the revolution of 1848, etc.? If immigration had been slower, the opening of the West as well as the rise of industry would have been delayed considerably.

But all this is hypothetical. It is certain that a new center arose here in America, much more powerful than the other non-European centers that we have reviewed so far. Nevertheless, one is justified in saying that its influence as a separate center, that is, not merely an extension of Europe, has been felt for only about forty or fifty years. America had her period of isolation, when she was neglected in the calculations of European statesmen, when she was disconnected from all European powers, and when she, consequently, did not add anything to anyone's might but seemed remote and unimportant enough not to be taken into consideration. American statesmen constructed a theory, almost a dogma, out of this fact — a theory which kept broad masses under its spell at a moment when the United States was heavily entangled in world affairs. The political view blinded most people to the undeniable facts of economic, and, as we shall see, of cultural life.

CHAPTER IV

Cultural Shift and Transformation in the Anglo-Saxon World

IN DISCUSSING the development of Latin America we noted an intermediate period of almost complete isolation — complete in the case of Spanish America. In the case of the British Dominions there was no such complete severance, although a considerable degree of separation, over a period, is to be noted in certain fields. In the field of foreign policy, for example, instead of a steadily growing influence, we see in the Dominions the desire to refrain from influencing imperial policy, growing out of fear of exposing themselves and of being finally overruled, as well as the desire to keep out of perilous entanglements and avoid responsibility. The First World War changed this attitude in the Dominions somewhat but did not end the internal strife between isolationists and those who consider the Dominions strong enough to influence imperial policy. We find the same attitude, even more pronounced, in the history of the political and institutional influence of the United States, particularly in foreign relations.

In the intellectual and cultural field there was also an intermediate period of separation. After the epoch when Benjamin Franklin, Benjamin Thomson, and the painters Benjamin West, Gilbert Stuart, and John Singleton Copley achieved fame on both sides of the Atlantic, there was a

long time when hardly an American, aside from some leading politicians, was known outside America.

On the other hand, the cultural contact was maintained
by the steady influx of English books and newspapers into
America. There was no cultural disruption comparable to
the break between Spain and her former colonies which
would have allowed another literature and civilization to
replace the English. This was true during a period when
French was generally the vehicle of higher education
throughout Europe. English literature was not popular in
Europe outside Great Britain during this period, but in
America English literature prevailed. This ratio of many
English books in America to hardly one American book in
Great Britain lasted into the twentieth century, and for some
categories of books has persisted until today.[1]

The necessity of devoting all power and ingenuity to
pioneer work in a newly settled country is so obvious that
the cultural lag of colonial areas does not need further explanation. Even at a later stage, when conditions have improved, the tradition of cultural inferiority hinders the real
appraisal of cultural values coming from such countries.
The Americans themselves only gradually lost the feeling
of being culturally a European colony. Although before
the middle of the nineteenth century some Americans became famous and influential outside their country, it was a
long way from the appreciation of such single men to the
acknowledgment that there existed a well-established Amer-

[1] Heindel, *The American Impact on Great Britain*, p. 317, says that
American books were easier to sell in the Dominions than in Great Britain,
and he quotes a publisher who sold five times as many copies of business
books in Germany and four times as many in Scandinavia and Holland as
in the United Kingdom. According to Miller and Hill, *The Giant of the
Western World*, p. 5, $9,000,000 worth of books were imported into the
United States in 1929, not counting translations and American editions.

ican civilization. Indeed men like Washington Irving, Emerson, Hawthorne, Edgar Allan Poe, and even Cooper, were hardly distinguishable as Americans. There is scarcely anything particularly American in their writings. It has been said that the first really American book was Mark Twain's *Huckleberry Finn*.[2] His humor and that of other authors after him is distinctly American, different from British and other European humor. Today there is no question but that there is a distinct spirit and distinct tradition in other fields of American literature also. The first American poets and scholars were followed by others in steadily increasing number.

The same stage was reached in most of the British Dominions at the beginning of the twentieth century, when a few persons were acknowledged as outstanding men but the emergence of new cultural centers was as yet realized but dimly and only by a few.[3]

The political influence of the Dominions grew along with their economic and numerical ascendancy. Political power may be won by nations which have only recently emerged to separate existence, while cultural maturity, on the other hand, is intimately connected with the existence of a traditional background.[4] Therefore, and only accidentally because of their broader demographic basis, the cultural center of gravity shifted much more to the United States than to the Dominions.

It is impossible to give an exact date for the rise of the

[2] Stephen Leacock, "The Future of American Humor," *St. Louis Post Dispatch*, Fiftieth Anniversary Number, Dec. 9, 1928.

[3] C. Hartley Grattan, *Introducing Australia*, p. 178, emphasizes "the vast importance of the nineties in Australian history."

[4] The lack of such a tradition is sometimes deplored for the United States. It is lacking even more in the Dominions. See Charles A. and Mary R. Beard, *America in Midpassage* (New York, 1939), II, 754.

new centers. But, considering the present situation, the fact itself is undeniable. We may open any English book, as often as not we shall find a non-European city given as the place of publication. Even more characteristic are those publishing firms which are located in two continents at the same time. Many books are published in "London–New York–Toronto," etc. Harvard, Yale, Princeton, Columbia, have as high standards as either Cambridge or Oxford in England. From the beginning of the twentieth century, at the very latest, Anglo-Saxon civilization has been no longer a predominantly European concern.

Moreover, at present it is not merely a matter of Britain and America, but of the Dominions as well. The University of Toronto, for example, ranks certainly not very far below the outstanding places of learning in Britain and the United States, and is considered at least on the same level as most of the younger universities in Britain and many American universities. Some Australian universities, Melbourne's, etc., have had a prodigious development during recent years. The population of New Zealand is only 1 per cent of that of the United States; the first whites came to New Zealand when Franklin had been dead for exactly half a century and when the fame of Poe, Washington Irving, and others had been established for some years; nevertheless, New Zealand is the birthplace of writers of well-established fame, such as Katherine Mansfield and Sir Hugh Walpole. Sir Ernest Rutherford is a New Zealander, and he carried through the work which brought him fame and the Nobel prize when he worked at McGill University in Canada. It may be noted that the most influential cartoonist in present-day England, David Low, came from New Zealand, and is perhaps one channel bringing some of the pioneer spirit into Britain which may be essential for the social transformation developing there during the present war. Australia has taken into her own hands the stupendous task of exploring her vast deserted interior, and has fulfilled that task with the same thoroughness and efficiency which European explorers of different origin displayed in Africa. Furthermore, Australia has explored those parts of Antarctica which are nearest to her territory. Sir Douglas Mawson, Sir Hubert Wilkins, and John Rymill rank among the outstanding living Antarctic explorers. Canada has furnished to the Empire statesmen internationally esteemed such as Sir Wilfrid Laurier, a French Canadian. Canada has also contributed an abundant share in medical research and in biological research: the developing of wheat adapted for dry areas with hot short summers was an achievement of immense value, not only for Canada; so was the discovery of insulin by Banting, Best, and Macleod. The South African leader, General Smuts, is of Boer origin. Thus, although there is no doubt that the cultural influence of the Dominions is much weaker than the cultural influence of the United States, and much weaker than their political influence, it is relatively strong, if the relatively small population and short history of the Dominions are taken into consideration.

Returning to the United States, we do not need to review here all the achievements of American scientists. But we shall cite some of those instances where American science and scholarship had influence on the development of the Western World, especially where this influence has become so continuous as to demonstrate quite clearly the shifting of the cultural center from Europe.

Both the philosophical school of Pragmatism and the psychological system of Behaviorism were born in America. Certainly philosophical thinking presupposes a cultural tradition and a social system allowing some gifted people to spend their time in thought. It is therefore clear that the conditions of a newly settled country struggling hard for mere existence are not favorable for philosophical or psychological studies. On the other hand, the matter-of-factness of the colonial atmosphere, the practical spirit of the Americans, their longing for practical success, opened the way for just these systems. The reaction to metaphysics is natural in a people who have gone through the school of pioneerdom, but that these schools of thought are not ways of thinking adapted only to colonial people with comparatively primitive needs is shown by their impact on European thought. Pragmatism as developed by William James [5] and John Dewey has found ardent followers in England since 1900 in the persons of F. C. S. Schiller and W. Caldwell. Behaviorism was accepted by Englishmen as well as in other parts of Europe; its outstanding investigator is perhaps the Russian, I. Pavlov. But one can say that both schools retained their center in America. Thus the twentieth century brought a shift of the center of balance from Europe overseas even in this lofty sphere.

We have already mentioned the fact that American writing through the medium of the common language began to influence British literature rather early in the nineteenth century, although American books did not constitute a conspicuous part of the literature sold on the British market before the end of the century. The influence upon other European literature was never so great. Still later, at the end of the century, American methods of education began

[5] Pragmatism as first taught by Pierce is a little older, but it became an influential school only through James.

to arouse attention in Europe. Here for the first time not Britain but Bolshevist Russia is the country most influenced. Not all the American educational principles that were discussed in Russian literature were adopted; some, such as the Dalton plan, were transformed; others were misunderstood. But the fact of the strong influence remains. Similarly, we find attempts to transplant the American educational system in its entirety to Australia.[6]

In the late 'nineties, when the educational influence was beginning to be felt, a similar development was seen in many other fields, notably in architecture, technology, commercial improvements, and foreign policy. In all these fields American influence had, at least in certain periods, a stronger impact on other European countries than on Britain. American technology was studied very thoroughly in Germany and Belgium, and after the Bolshevist revolution, in Russia. Perhaps no other country acknowledged American technological leadership as willingly as Bolshevist Russia. But, reluctantly or not, all European countries opened themselves to American influence.

Among the first scholarly researches known outside America were historical studies. Of the works in this field Prescott's famous *History of the Reign of Ferdinand and Isabella* is the very first historical work of an American which opened new sources and enjoyed an international reputation.[7] Since its publication there has been no decade in which American historians have not produced works internationally recognized. To these individual achievements must be added the results of collective researches, such as the excavations in the Near and the Far East.

[6] Fred Alexander, *Australia and the United States*, p. 13.
[7] G. P. Gooch, *History and Historians in the Nineteenth Century* (London, 1913), p. 413.

American medicine is another example of a science which began to influence European theory and practice at least a century ago. From the first application of anaesthetics by Morton and Jackson in 1845 to the Nobel prize winners Minot–Murphy–Whipple and their treatment of blood-diseases, and the brain surgery of Harvey Cushing, American medical science has never ceased to produce men who have influenced European science. Especially illuminating are improvements where the initial invention has been made in Europe, but the full impact could be felt only after American technological genius had made them usable on a large scale. DDT was discovered in European laboratories. But its use in treating whole islands and ridding them from the scourge of malaria is at least as great a step forward in preventive medicine as any. The case of penicillin is somewhat similar, as its effectiveness was recognized in England but American pharmaceutic laboratories produced it in great quantities for the first time. It came to many European countries, such as Germany and Italy, as a gift from America. A particular instance is that of American dentistry, which invaded Europe not only intellectually, but materially. Especially in Britain, France, and Italy, the American dentist was a well-known person, and many native dentists thought it necessary to advertise that they used American methods. As early as 1873 an American Dental Society of Europe was founded.

On the other hand, there are fields in which America did not attract international attention before the twentieth century. For example, a science which is today one of the most outstanding in America, astronomy, showed results relatively late. There were respectable American astronomers in the 'thirties of the nineteenth century, but the leading position of American astronomy was attained only about 1900. The technical progress which is responsible for the building and equipping of the Lick Observatory and the observatory on Mount Wilson with its spectacular lens gave American astronomers such a tremendous advantage that most of the more important discoveries of the last years have been made in the United States. The technical development has coincided with the emergency of a generation of astronomers well prepared in their scientific education.

Our main task, however, is not to evaluate the achievements of the Americans or other non-Europeans, but to point out that they have begun to constitute centers of civilization and learning to break the monopoly of Europe. The existence of scholars and artists in an unbroken chain is the indispensable condition, but their existence alone does not warrant the shift of the center of gravity. It may point to a tendency toward shift, not more. It is, therefore, important to note that Europe only very lately has begun to recognize the existence of an active cultural center in America. The first lectures on American history were delivered at Oxford as late as 1912. Some individuals, it is true, realized America's importance very early, but they remained isolated individuals; Freeman, the great English historian, regretted eighty years ago that many people were aware of the impact of the French Revolution, but only a few of that of the American Revolution.

In reviewing scientific achievements one may forget sometimes the diversity of nations and be impressed by the fact of the unity of Western science. There is no doubt that the British Dominions as well as the United States belong to this Western civilization. But as we have stressed in other respects, they are nevertheless individual nations.

Among Americans, Arthur M. Schlesinger just recently discussing "the American" said that, though "probably none of the traits is peculiar to the American people, the sum total represents a way of life unlike that of any other nation." [8] And among foreigners, Carr-Saunders may be cited as saying [9] that Americans constitute a nation because their ways, customs, and manners are quite distinct, as English, French, and German ways are. Their approach to matters of daily concern and their outlook upon them are more or less uniform throughout the whole population of the United States and differ more from those of any of the Western European nations than those of the latter differ from each other.

If Canada, Australia, and New Zealand are not yet nations in the same degree they are without doubt nations in the making. It may be sufficient to deal with their cultural role briefly. It is a matter of dispute whether Canadians, Australians, and New Zealanders are nearer the British or the Americans in their approach to matters of daily concern. [10] Many Canadians stress their similarity to the British; others, though loyal to Britain politically, will contest such a view energetically. In general Canadians who have spent considerable time in the United States will stress their affinity to the British in their more refined manners; while Canadians returning from the British Isles will often stress the freer life in Canada that is similar to the American way of life.

In Australia and New Zealand customs and manners have retained more of the particular British flavor. But here also

[8] Arthur M. Schlesinger, "What then is the American, This New Man?" *American Historical Review*, XVIII, 244 (January 1943).

[9] Alexander M. Carr-Saunders, "Europe Overseas," in Julian S. Huxley, *We Europeans* (London, 1935), pp. 253–257.

[10] Several examples in McCormac, *Canada; America's Problem*, p. 148.

the pioneering stage has favored a directness in speech and manners, a certain heartiness combined with a certain roughness.[11] British ways and traditions persist, but are liberated, as it were, from certain inhibitions. British ideas and ideals prevail, but perhaps with more of the vehemence of youth. British economic and political methods continue, but modified by a new physical environment and the uncertainty and inexperience entailed. Democracy takes very concrete, and sometimes novel, forms.[12] Novel forms are especially conspicuous in the social democracy of New Zealand. The New Zealand Social Security Act had definite influence on the shaping of the Beveridge Plan in Great Britain.[13] Indeed all these new nations, Americans, Canadians, Australians, New Zealanders, share this democratic spirit, arising from the conditions of the laborious, dangerous, lonely frontier life. The early attempts of the British to transplant their class institutions to some American and Australian colonies were of no avail.

Modern Western civilization is generally distinguished from other and older civilizations by the literacy of the masses. Education is no longer a privilege, though the extent varies widely within every nation. Pioneer countries are characterized by having no group of people whose education is much above the average. There is no time and energy left for achieving higher education. This is a feature of America shared with other colonial and pioneer countries

[11] Alexander, p. 11.

[12] O. H. T. Rishbeth, an Australian living in England, in the *Encyclopaedia Britannica* (14th ed., 1938), II, 735.

[13] Sir William Beveridge, in his report on *Social Security and Allied Services* (American edition, New York, 1942), acknowledges only the influences of the New Zealand scheme and denies every other foreign influence.

even in a period of her history when she could hardly be called a colonial country any longer. But she differed from other countries of that type by the absence of a large group of uneducated illiterate people. Later on, when America had developed her own intellectual centers prepared to take a place among the intellectual centers of Western civilization, the prejudice towards her colonial backwardness for a long time prevented Europeans as well as Americans from acknowledging her high standing. The stream of students and scholars from Europe to America was only a trickle compared with the number of Americans going to European places of learning, even in the twentieth century.[14] Most of the foreign students in the United States came from the Far East, some from Canada and Latin America. There were only a few teachers in higher education in America who did not visit Europe at least once in their lifetime, but of European teachers only specialists in American history, geography, economics, etc., considered it worth while to visit the United States. More scholars came from the British Isles, relatively very few from the European continent. One may conclude from this state of affairs that in regard to education [15] the shifting of the center of balance from Europe to other continents has not yet started. This is true in even greater degree for the British Dominions and South America. But the increasing number of students coming from Latin America and the Far East to the United States [16]

[14] Heindel, p. 275, says that from 1925 to 1939 only 2558 students came from England, relatively more from Ireland. When he mentions 2673 foreign students in the United States in the year 1904, we may suppose that most of them came from non-European countries.

[15] This is true only for educational practice. For educational theory compare what is said on page 101.

[16] In 1930, of the 1484 Chinese students who applied for passports to go to foreign schools, 55.6 per cent wanted to go to Japan, 18 per cent

– and to Canada also – shows a change in attitude towards the United States and Canada, if not in Europe, at least in the mother countries of these students. More and more experts are summoned from America to these countries – experts in aviation, roadbuilding, soil conservation, flood control, engineering, etc. World War II gave a notable impulse to this development. Before 1939 technical experts of all kinds had been summoned to countries such as Turkey or Iran, but the number of students they sent to America remained negligible. In 1941 the Turkish Government transferred 92 technical students from German and British institutions to American ones. In 1946 the number had increased to 178. The same year saw 17,000 foreign students altogether in American institutions.

The widespread literacy, the technical progress, and, relatively speaking, the absence of a higher-educated class which could or would like to monopolize the opportunities for influence and entertainment, all make it understandable that America has taken the leading part in the evolution of the press and the movies. Even on the stage, though in a smaller degree, the American impact made itself felt about 1900, especially in the United Kingdom.

The evolution of the moving picture from its beginning by Edison to its present development in the talkies is almost completely American. Backed by the great internal market, the American film industry can produce more and cheaper films than any competitor.[17] And still more important is

---

to the United States, 11.6 per cent to France; the United States was the goal for as many students as all European countries together, the Soviet Union excluded. Figures from Kenneth Scott Latourette, *The Chinese; Their History and Culture* (New York, 1934), p. 490. Pearl Harbor left more than 1000 Chinese students stranded in the United States.

[17] John Eugene Harley, *The World Wide Influence of the Cinema*

the fact that America has used her technical superiority to develop a center of influence in Hollywood. Actors, writers, and musicians from all countries of the world have been attracted to that center and have begun to work from there. It is unaccountable how efficiently, though slowly, the American way of life has influenced manners, customs, habits, and valuations of other peoples. It has even helped to spread the knowledge of English. Students of modern Ireland consider the movies a very important factor for the perpetuation of the English language in Eire.[18] What in former centuries missionaries, merchants, sailors, did in bringing European clothes, etc., to foreign peoples, the American movie does much more thoroughly and swiftly. It acts more strongly upon the Europeans than upon non-Europeans, and among Europeans upon the English-speaking ones.[19] The influence is smaller in other countries, where the pictures alone must convey the meaning or those few films whose success is so big that it seems profitable to translate them are given in a synchronized version. How strongly and insensibly this influence works may be illustrated by a single quotation: "Several of these [American] usages have since come to be so frequent in this country that scarcely any Englishman regards them to-day as importa-

---

(Los Angeles, 1940), p. 21, states that the United States produces 65 per cent of all films.

[18] Tom Ireland, *Ireland; Past and Present*, p. 542, describes the influence of the American movies. Many young people trying to imitate movie celebrities of Irish origin become accustomed to typical American manners, even to American slang.

[19] Southard, *American Industry in Europe*, p. 102. In 1929, 75 per cent of the English market was served by American films, but only 48 per cent of the French and 33 per cent of the German market. The year 1929 is chosen as a date prior to the governmental regulation which later took place in most European countries.

tions." [20]   In most European languages, expressions from
American slang such as "boss," "O.K.," "gangster," etc.,
have become familiar in their original form through the
movies, while formerly Americanisms were adopted in a
translated form, as "gratte-ciel," "gratta-nuvole," or "Wol-
kenkratzer" for skyscraper, and "Hinterwaeldler" for back-
woodsman. Other words have been taken over in their
original form, such as "canoe," "yankee," etc., though no
longer given their original pronunciation, thus revealing
the literary route of transmission.

The influence of the American press lies much more on
the technical side. American news agencies furnish material
to the European press, but only in relatively inconspicuous proportion. Even in this respect, however, America
is driving Europe from her position as center of information, since American news agencies have replaced the
European especially in South America and the Far East.
From 1883 on, an American newspaper, the *New York
Herald*, has had a separate European edition, edited in Paris.

The movement to reduce the cost of newspapers started
more than a hundred years ago in the United States and
was brought to Europe only in the second half of the nineteenth century. But newspapers even then remained rather
expensive. In 1883 Joseph Pulitzer bought the *New York
World*, transformed it into a cheap paper, and made it interesting for people who were not used to reading. Hearst
and his yellow press followed soon, and so, some time later,
did the "Boulevard press" of Paris and Berlin. It is not by
mere chance that August Scherl, the owner and editor of
the *Berliner Lokalanzeiger*, one of the first cheap European

[20] Herbert W. Horwill, *A Dictionary of Modern American Usage*
(Oxford, 1935), Preface, p. ix.

newspapers, had his first journalistic training in America.[21] American "sensationalism" and "degeneration" were first scorned, but at last taken over. Other features also of the American press infiltrated. When Robert P. Porter returned from America, he introduced the famous supplements into the London *Times*.[22] A feature which was accepted only to a minor degree by the European press was the interview; but it became not unusual for European statesmen, artists, etc., to influence European public opinion by interviews granted to American journalists.[23]

Even before the movies became such a powerful instrument of propaganda, American influence in shaping public opinion was to be felt, especially in Great Britain. During the last quarter of the nineteenth century, in the "generation of materialism," [24] the assault on traditional religion reached its climax. The most widespread propaganda in the English-speaking world came from America, where Lester Ward edited his vehemently anti-religious journal. It is difficult to ascertain how far his journal and the writings of other Americans were of influence. Distrusting American leadership in other respects at this time, it yet seems that Europeans were ready to accept American leadership in such a popular movement. The American anti-religious movement slowed down rather soon, while in Europe the socialist parties took it over and spread it among the working classes. In America, modernism, and its opposite, fundamentalism, became much more characteristic, especially among Prot-

[21] Carlton J. H. Hayes, *A Generation of Materialism, 1870–1900* (New York, 1941), p. 179.
[22] Heindel, pp. 12 ff.
[23] The word "interview" and derivations from it became familiar in many European languages, e.g. *interviewer* in French, *interviewen* in German.   [24] Hayes, pp. 128–129.

estants and Jews. New sects such as Mormons and Christian Scientists spread and started missionary work even in Europe, followed by older sects, who had lived until this period only within the United States. Quakers and Mormons won members in different countries, although not in conspicuous numbers. Much larger is the number of Christian Scientists in Europe.[25] The American Methodist Church has even appointed bishops for some European countries. Particularly strong was the influence in Great Britain and primarily in the Nonconformist churches. "To those who have been brought up in the sectarian seclusion of the Anglican cult, it is difficult to realize the extent to which American books, American preachers, American hymnody, moulded the lives of the Free Churches of this country."[26] The revivals of the late nineteenth century were not the offspring of the old Wesleyan methods, but were brought back from America in modernized form. It may be doubtful whether the religious influence of America on Europe is really strong; certainly there is no such influence in the non-Protestant European countries, either Catholic or Greek Orthodox. But, strong or weak, there was American religious influence on Europe during a period when Europe — again outside the Catholic church — had almost ceased to influence religious thought in America. During the same period American missions grew in numbers. This growth was due to the financial backing they had through many individuals throughout the States as well as to the widespread missionary zeal. It is no wonder that a similarly growing number of people in the Far East and also

[25] Miller and Hill, pp. 94 and 207, estimate the number of Christian Scientist churches in Europe at 250 and state that the *Christian Science Monitor* had a daily output of 10,000 copies in Europe.

[26] W. T. Stead, quoted by Heindel, p. 364.

in Africa began to look toward America as one center of the Western World.

In the twentieth century Americans and Britons, perhaps the latter more than the former, have begun to become more conscious of their "common Anglo-Saxon civilization." The fact that a big percentage of Americans are of non-British parentage has never been forgotten, but the "melting pot" has seemed to produce a thorough Americanization characterized by the common English language. Besides, the masses of immigrants from other countries have belonged at least in the first generation to the poorest and most poorly educated classes. Although the second generation was supposed to be sufficiently assimilated it played no conspicuous part among the leaders of American civilization. Indeed, except for a few old families of Dutch origin, such as those of the presidents Van Buren and Roosevelt, and a few German political emigrants of 1848, such as Carl Schurz, American civilization until recently has been represented almost entirely by men of Anglo-Saxon stock.

This situation changed at the very moment when people on both sides of the Atlantic were beginning to stress the Anglo-Saxon character of American civilization.[27] Two of the American Nobel Prize winners, K. Landsteiner and A. A. Michelson, were immigrants, Austrian and German Jews. Mayors of the two biggest American cities, New York and Chicago, have had Italian and Czech names respectively. The recent revolutions in Europe have brought to America an unprecedented number of intellectuals — writers of fame, scholars of international reputation, among

[27] This change did not pass unnoticed, however. See the quotation in Mencken, *The American Language*, p. 476, from the London *Nation*, March 12, 1912.

them several Nobel Prize winners: Thomas Mann and
Albert Einstein from Germany, the Joliot-Curies from
France, Sigrid Undset from Norway, the famous physicist
Fermi, the conductor Toscanini, the historian Salvemini
from Italy, the philosopher Maritain from France, and
Bruno Walter from Austria, to name only a few.[27a] We may
add that the First World war also brought a certain number,
though smaller, of outstanding men to America — the Polish
pianist Paderewski, the Russian violinist Jascha Heifetz, the
composer Sergei Rachmaninoff, and the conductor Koussevitzky among them. It may be noted that the number of
foreigners among singers and musicians has been great all
through the last decades. This only shows how complicated
a process the shift of balance is. There are spheres where
the center of gravity lay on European soil until the present
war.

This lag in the development of a musical center may
account also for the fact that in 1930 only two broadcasts
were sent from America for every hundred coming from
Great Britain to America. In 1936 the ratio remained
favorable to Great Britain, although rapidly changing,
thirty-six to one hundred.[28] A competent critic, however,
considers that by now America has gone through the preliminary stages of importing musicians and music, that she
has already produced her own musicians, supreme in inter-
preting foreign music.[29] He sees America "entering the
third period, wherein the quantity and quality of our

[27a] The flight of Nazi scholars after this war brought and may bring
some more German scientists and scholars to South America, though the
British are at present preventing Werner Heisenberg, the Nobel prize
winner for physics, from accepting an offer in Buenos Aires.

[28] Heindel, p. 334.

[29] Beard, II, 759, quoting Roy Harris.

musicians and our audiences demand a new native music, conceived in the mood and the tempo of our time." He concedes an exception only for conductors. And Sergei Koussevitzky himself said after his return from a European trip in 1937: "European composers have simply nothing to say. Our American composers are consistently better artists." [30]

The same is true in most arts, including painting; America has produced some painters of well-deserved fame. But even these did not influence European painting. American painting remained dependent on European schools. Many American painters studied in England, France, or Italy; many lived there a great part of their adult lives. For a short time, from the 'nineties — the critical period in so many respects — to the end of the next decade, a school of New York artists began to paint the "American scene." But before they succeeded in attracting attention from Europe this impulse was lost, when Cézanne and the postimpressionists became known in America. Again Paris lured the American painters away, both spiritually and physically. Only the great depression of 1929, the impossibility for even foreigners to produce independently in the states ruled by dictators, and finally the Second World War forced them back to America. When these artists returned home they found a slightly changed atmosphere. While in former periods Americans had bought works of art indiscriminately, these very collections, munificently opened to the public, had made possible a more understanding appreciation of art. Well-directed museums in some large cities and the influence of the European intellectual immigration created one condition for raising a new American art. Al-

[30] Quoted in Beard, II, 760.

though expositions of the very recent years reveal that most American painters could easily be classified with one or another of the different European schools, an increasing number of artists like to choose American motives and scenes, a fact pointing to the development of a distinct American school. This development is a necessary preliminary stage before American painting can possibly influence painters abroad. This is one of the very few instances where the Latin-American center has decidedly left the American center behind.

Of all the arts, only architecture has been so highly developed in America as to influence other countries. American, like Latin-American, architecture had already developed its own style in colonial times, a style slightly different from the English, altered by the use of timber instead of stone or brick. The primitive colonial life, the absence of splendid churches and palaces, gave to colonial American architecture a beautiful simplicity. This colonial style has been preserved, only slightly changed, until today. The role which the French cultural influence played in Latin American, the classic Greek-Roman example played in North American architecture. Other styles followed, but while architects like Richardson created valuable and characteristic buildings, they did not influence Europe in any way. Only when steel and concrete made it possible to solve problems previously unheard of did Europe begin to look towards American architecture. The Brooklyn Bridge, built in 1883, stimulated imitation abroad. It is true that the first skyscrapers, although tremendous technical achievements, lacked artistic qualities. But during the same period American architects learned to use steel and concrete in plants, power-houses, silos, etc., and from these artistically unpretentious buildings a new style, a "functional architecture," arose. Now houses too were built in this "glass and girder" architecture. More recently many American architects have learned to master not only the technical problems of the skyscrapers, but the aesthetic problems also.

Again we can see the phenomenon already mentioned: *The development of a real national style did not lead to increasing isolation, but to the re-integration of America into Western civilization. America became a new center.* The new apartment houses built first in the Netherlands and then throughout Europe were not directly copies from American styles, but were strongly influenced by them. Russia after the Bolshevist revolution built her factories and dams after the American pattern; skyscrapers and bridges were built in Australia as well as in Japan, but would never have been built without the American examples, and sometimes with the active coöperation of Americans.

American civilization, there can be no doubt, is part of Western civilization, but it has branched away from every European variety of that civilization. However greatly customs may differ in different parts of the territory of the United States, the differences from European customs are yet more striking. These differences tended to increase so long as America was somewhat backward and did not influence Europe. This has been the case in South America until the present day. The differences between America and Europe have decreased in proportion to America's growing influence on Europe. One striking example may be cited, the evolution of the language. The well-known critic, H. L. Mencken, stated in the first three editions of his book on the American language that it is deviating from the English language. In the fourth edition, 1936, he said: "The Englishman, of late, has yielded so much to American example in vocabulary, in idiom, in spelling, and even in pronunciation, that what he speaks promises to become . . . a kind of dialect of American, just as the language spoken by the Americans was once a dialect of English." [31] And elsewhere he stated: "The Englishman, whether he knows it or not, is talking and writing more and more American. He becomes so accustomed to it that he grows unconscious of it. . . . The influence of 125,000,000 people, practically all headed in one direction, is simply too great to be resisted by any minority, however resolute." [32]

To realize fully all the implications of this American cultural development, it ought to be seen in its different aspects: as a descendant of European Western civilization, as a part of the Anglo-Saxon civilization embracing Great Britain, the United States, and the Dominions, and as one of the new centers, a little ahead of the others, but not so much so as to constitute a difference in principle.

We should like to repeat once more: America has become a cultural center within the area of Western civilization. Nevertheless the slogan, "Americanization of the World," is misleading. Competing cultural centers are undoubtedly arising in the British Dominions and in Latin America. Their emergence has often been minimized because they did not constitute such tremendous demographic, economic, and political power. They seemed to lag in their cultural development not only behind Europe, but behind the United States. But the American center also is very young. It is not even yet a center in all cultural activities. The lag of other competing centers, therefore, is not really

[31] Mencken, quoted by Heindel, p. 3.
[32] Mencken, p. 31.

great. Latin America emerged as a potential cultural center rather suddenly in 1898. But the 'nineties are also decisive for the emergence of the American center. Here the shift developed more gradually. The same gradual shift is recognizable in the constitutional development of the British Dominions. In view of the epoch-making importance of the Spanish-American War of 1898, it is rather surprising that the First World War marked a new stage for America only in power politics — and not even that for the other new centers; in all cultural respects it represented only an acceleration of the development, in other respects not even that — for instance, in the shift of centers of some sciences. It is still too early to assess the lasting influence of World War II. It may mark the complete collapse of the European centers or it may slow down their development. Development of the non-European centers has been accelerated, and there is no reason why this trend should not continue. The cultural come-back in some European countries has been surprising. Since 1945 more artistic films have been produced in France, Britain, and Italy than in America or Russia. European museums have been able to display their treasures more effectively. Stage and opera have experienced a renaissance even in places as badly damaged as Vienna. But some cultural losses are irreplaceable: irreparable damage was done to architectural monuments in German, Polish, and Italian cities such as Nürnberg, Warsaw, and Florence. British scientific journals still are unable to print other than very short articles. Many of the German [33]

[33] E.g. of the twenty-odd German geographical reviews, some of world-wide reputation, none has yet resumed publication, and they have been replaced by only one new magazine. See Eric Fischer, "A German Geographer Reviews German Geography," *Geographical Review*, April, 1948.

and some other scientific publications are dead. Even a complete recovery would mean the loss of precious years during which non-European nations are forging ahead. Many Americans have only lately realized that Europe will not resume its economic and political position automatically and as a matter of course. In cultural matters the same fact is hardly yet realized.

CHAPTER V

Russia's Shift to Asia

W<small>E HAVE DISCUSSED</small> from several different points of view the gradual shift of the center of balance from certain parts of Europe to other parts of the world. This may enable us to recognize a tendency toward a similar shift in countries where such a movement has started only recently. Among these nations Russia is the most important, not because of the political power of the Soviet Union, but because of the numerous Russians who live under the same political rule outside of the conventional boundaries of the European continent. The number of Irish, Italians, etc., living overseas may be equally important, but their political status is different. Though we do not want to overrate the importance of population numbers as a cause for the shifting of the center, demographic changes are, nevertheless, an indispensable presupposition.

We have noted that in some respects the United States influenced Great Britain most strongly, in other respects other countries earlier and even more strongly. It sounds paradoxical, but is nevertheless undeniable, that the Soviet Union, though most remote in its ideas and ideals, is quite exceptionally fascinated by America, especially by her technical standards and achievements in organization, but also by certain things in the intellectual sphere, as, for example, educational ideas.

One may perhaps trace this susceptibility to some similar

conditions. It is obvious that there are many more diversities; thus we are warned from the very beginning not to overrate the similarities. Russia bears in many respects the clear signs of a young nation, a nation which settled in its present environment only a relatively short time ago. It may not be obvious to everybody how extensively Russia draws from a colonial past. Even most Russians are not consciously aware of this particular underlying reason for many peculiarities. The Americans cherish their colonial tradition consciously, even in those Eastern states which have a tradition of several centuries, older than the living tradition in some European, especially Balkan, countries. The "pioneer spirit" is felt in Russia too, even when not avowed. Only the Western Ukraine and the area around Novgorod have a history comparable in length and continuity to that of other European countries. Moscow is located on originally colonial soil. When the first Russian settlers came, the region was thickly forested and inhabited by a sparse population of Ugro-Finnish descent, related to the tribes of the present Northern Siberia, who played in Russian history a part similar to that of the Indians in America. Hopelessly outnumbered, culturally on a low level, they had to recede into the virgin forests or to succumb in the struggle with the Russians. The swiftest progress, however, was made in the most northern regions, which attracted enterprising people by their treasure of fur-bearing animals. This penetration to the northeast by trappers, fur-traders, and a few settlers lasted uninterruptedly for centuries. It is roughly comparable to the penetration of Canada by the agents of the Hudson's Bay Company and French trappers, and in its later stages is still contemporary with the American development. Russian fur hunters met those of the Hudson's Bay Company in the Oregon country in the nineteenth century.

In the thirteenth century the largest part of Russia was conquered by the Mongols or Tatars, and it remained a devastated and depopulated dependency of the Tatars for two and a half centuries. At that period there came into the Russian character and Russia governmental practice those Asiatic traits which are characteristic even to the present day. When Russia cast off the Mongolian yoke, the political center of a rather restricted national territory was around Moscow on "colonial soil." The historic center of Kiev remained under Polish domination for some centuries longer.

The sixteenth century witnessed a new Russian colonization towards the south, southeast, and east. The pioneers were merchants who traveled and settled along the great streams flowing to the Black Sea and the Caspian Sea. The wide plains filled slowly with Cossacks. These were originally peasants escaping from the political and economic oppression of the great landowners and the Czars, comparable in many respects to early American frontier folk coming from poverty-stricken or feudal European rural districts. The military conquest in most cases followed these early settlers, preceding them only in those areas where strong political societies hindered the advance of small groups.

The first large Russian colonization of the Volga Valley took place later than the first wave of Spanish settlers in America. Kuibyshev, the former Samara and substitute capital of the Soviet Union during the present war, was founded on newly conquered territory only five years before Raleigh's colony came to Roanoke Island. About the same time the conquest of Siberia started. When James-town in Virginia was founded, the Russians reached the upper Ob, and about the same time that the Pilgrims landed in New England the Russians reached the Yenisei. The colonization of Southern Russia went on more slowly. Kharkov became a Ukrainian city late in the sixteenth century, and the Don and the Donets basin were held by free Cossacks, but not yet included in the Russian Empire. Only after the American Revolution did the northern coast of the Black Sea become completely Russian. On the whole, European Russia was conquered but only partly settled at the end of the eighteenth century. Tatars and other "for-eign tribes" remained in the territory and were Russianized only slowly and to a small extent. The Russian coloniza-tion lasted in varying intensity during the whole of the nineteenth century. Large areas of European Russia were settled by a European population even later than some of the western states of the United States.

In the conquest of Central Asia, of the Caucasus, and of the far eastern provinces the governmental power often took the lead. But even here we find Russian merchants and sometimes peasants fleeing from serfdom in Russia as the forerunners of the conquest. The actual mass colonization of all the Asiatic provinces did not begin before the 1860's, when the peasants were freed from bondage. Political and criminal exiles were often the leading elements in the open-ing of new trades, small factories, etc., but the mass of workers and peasants were free migrants from Russia. In 1890 the Russian emigration to Siberia since the beginning of the century was estimated at about 2,500,000.[1] These

[1] Carr-Saunders, *World Population*, p. 56, seems to be the best author-ity. He estimates that between 1800 and 1900, some 3,700,000 emigrants

migrants mingled with the old Cossack pioneers and with
some native tribes. In Central Asia the Russian immigration
remained quite small, because the climate was not so attractive for European peasants. For this reason and because of
the Islamic faith of the natives, assimilation was incomplete.
The development in the Caucasus in some parts, especially
in the northern steppes, followed the Siberian pattern; in
others, especially the real mountain area, more the Central
Asiatic pattern.

In 1891 the Russians began to construct the Trans-
Siberian Railway. This made possible not only a more
extensive migration, but the export of Siberian products.
About the same time the Siberian Geological Society in
Tomsk began a series of explorations. Many deposits of
useful minerals were discovered. Leather and iron industries started in small workshops. A law issued by the
Minister Count Tolstoy provided the legal basis for migration by permitting the sale of personal shares of the community soil in the coöperative villages of Old Russia. The
migration developed swiftly and brought 400,000 persons
to Siberia between 1887 and 1894, or an average of 50,000
a year.[2] A few years later the estimated yearly average of
emigrants to Russian Asia was 100,000. A new epoch was
opened when the war against Japan led many thousands of
peasant soldiers over the Siberian railway. They saw the
fertile and empty country, and no propaganda could have

---

went into Russian Asia. But his account is hardly to be reconciled with
the figures of Charles Stéber, *La Sibérie et l'Extrême Nord Soviétique*
(Paris, 1936), p. 36. Stéber's figures are very reliable in general, but he
puts the total of emigrants from Russia to Siberia for 1860–85 at only
300,000, i.e., a yearly average of 12,000. He counts, it is true, only the
registered emigrants.

[2] *Cambridge Modern History*, XII, 318.

been so effective as this personal experience. In the next years, up to the First World War, the emigration rose to an average of a third of a million a year.[3]

The years of war and revolution, however important for the political development of Russian Asia, did not favor the growth of population or economic advance. Under the Bolshevist regime a rapid development of both began. Especially when the First Five-Year Plan was started, the development of Siberia, the Ural region, Turkestan, and the Caucasus stood foremost.[4] From the beginning the leading Soviet circles favored the development of industries far away from the frontiers in order to avoid the danger of enemy occupation and bombardment from the air. This military point of view was supported by the fact that many of the richest mines of different ores lay in the Ural area; iron here and in the Altai, coal in Southern Siberia in the Kusnetzk region and in central Kazakstan, gold in central Siberia, petroleum in the Caucasus and in the steppes of Kazakstan. A German economist and shrewd observer stated that the Soviets were able to carry through their program of "socialism within one country" only through industrialization connected with shifting the center of production to the East.[5] Central Asia and Turkestan became important for tropical products, particularly cotton. To save large areas for cotton Siberia had to enlarge her wheat-growing area, and a new railroad, the famous Turksib, had

[3] The statements differ widely. The figure in the text is accepted by the majority of authors. Carr-Saunders, p. 56, gives 3,500,000 as the total of the immigrants from 1900 to 1914; the average of the first half of this period is much below that for the second half.

[4] Together with some Ukrainian centers which seemed indispensable notwithstanding their strategically dangerous location.

[5] Paul Berkenkopf, *Siberien als Zukunftsland der Industrie* (Stuttgart, 1935), p. 10.

to be constructed to connect these two regions. In later
extensive railroad building the construction of a second
track on the Trans-Siberian Railroad and the construction
of a parallel railroad in Western Siberia and in the Far East
are to be mentioned. All construction involved skilled
laborers, engineers, and railroad personnel, but a large number of peasants were also brought to Siberia. New cities of
ten to a hundred thousand inhabitants developed eventually,
where formerly only treeless empty plains or thick woods
had been found. Old towns doubled, trebled, and even
further increased in population. It is said that industrial
production increased 277 per cent in Central Asia and 285
per cent in Siberia within the decade beginning with the
start of the First Five-Year Plan.[6] When the geological
survey discovered coal in the Aldan region, only 300 people lived there. It took a long time to complete a road to
this secluded spot, but when the road was finished, 30,000
people were living there. Within the next two years the
road brought another 18,000 people.[7] Stalinsk, the new
steel center in the Kusnetzk region, was founded in a territory then virtually uninhabited, and is at present a place of
170,000 inhabitants.[8] These developments certainly indi-

[6] Soviet statistics.
[7] Berkenkopf, p. 88.
[8] According to the census returns of January 1, 1939 (*The New International Yearbook*, 1941). The census of 1926 counted in the newly
founded settlement only 3,894 persons. Almost all large cities in Siberia,
the Caucasus, and Central Asia doubled their population between 1926
and 1939. The biggest non-European city of the Soviet Union, the fifth
in size, is Baku, which grew from 453,000 inhabitants in 1926 to 809,000
in 1939. Novosibirsk, the capital of the West Siberian region, was founded
under the name of Novonikolaevsk, when the Trans-Siberian Railroad
reached this spot. A few years later, in 1896, it already had 5,000 inhabitants (Arved Schultz, *Sibirien*, Breslau, 1923, p. 75). When it became the
capital of the West Siberian region the number jumped to 120,000 in
1926, 278,000 in 1933, 405,000 in 1939. Sverdlovsk (formerly called Ekate-

cate an important urbanization; but at the same time the
agricultural population has more than doubled. In 1897
about 5,227,000 people lived in all Siberia; [9] the census of
January 1, 1930, gave 8,250,000 people in Western Siberia,
2,800,000 people in Eastern Siberia, among them only 15
per cent urban population.[10] As a result of rapid industrialization and its concomitants the rural population of the
Soviet Union decreased by 5 per cent between 1926 and
1939. Only the 8 Soviet Republics of Central Asia and the
Caucasus showed an increase of 19 to 36 per cent. The
Urals, Siberia, Bashkiria, and the Far East, had a stationary
rural population, which signifies a strong relative decrease.[10a] Though figures are not available, it is safe to conclude from other reports that demands of the army and of
war industries rather strengthened this trend. The total
population of Siberia plus that of Russian Central Asia comprised 31,000,000 people in 1939. To that number we must

---

rinburg), one of the few older towns, the center of the Ural region, had
in 1926, a population of 136,000; in 1939, 426,000 inhabitants. Cheliabinsk,
near Sverdlovsk, also on the Asiatic side of the Ural, grew from 59,000 to
273,000; and Magnitogorsk, in the mountains, which had only thirty-
seven families of semi-nomadic herders in 1926 (Harry Peter Smolka,
40,000 against the Arctic, New York, 1937, p. 38), had in 1939, 145,000 inhabitants. (All figures, where not otherwise stated, are taken from *The
Statesman's Yearbook*, 1941, and *The New International Yearbook*, 1941.)
Of the 49 "boom cities," those of more than 50,000 population showing
an increase threefold or more between 1926 and 1939, 13 are located in
the Urals–Kusnetzk–Karaganda triangle, 4 farther east, and 4 in Central
Asia. (Frank Lorimer, *The Population of the Soviet Union: History and
Prospects* [League of Nations, Geneva, 1946], p. 147.)

[9] The census returns for Jan. 28, 1896, gave only 22,000,000 inhabitants
for all Asiatic territories of Russia: 9,250,000 in the Caucasus, 7,750,000 in
Central Asia.

[10] In 1912 there were 8,000,000 peasants in Siberia and 1,500,000 merchants, members of the army, officials, clerks, and convicts (Schultz,
p. 162). The figures are not strictly comparable, as many of the second
group of categories lived in rural settlements.

[10a] Lorimer, p. 157.

add the 8,000,000 of the three Transcaucasian Soviet republics, an unspecified number in other Caucasian regions, and the population of the Ural region. A part of this region was formerly included in the area of Siberia,[11] but the greater part of the former European Ural was in Czarist times very sparsely settled. We may, therefore, put the population of newly settled colonial soil outside European Russia proper as at least 45,000,000, or about one-fourth of the total Soviet citizenship.[12]

The Third Five-Year Plan increased the tempo of settling, building of new communications, and setting up of new industries. In the second year of this plan the present war broke out. Although exact information for the last years is not available, the main trend is clear enough. The growth of Russian industry and population has intensified. This has been possible because it developed along lines which were planned long before. There is a change in only one important respect. In the years preceding the war, new industries were built up in Russian Asia in addition to old and even new ones in European Russia. The new installations of the war years in Soviet Asia are not new establishments, but whole plants, moved with their machinery and most of their engineers and skilled workers.[13] The handicap of the older

[11] Erich Thiel, *Verkehrsgeographie von Russisch Asien* (Koenigsberg-Berlin, 1934), p. 31, referring to 1931, gives 1,910,000 inhabitants for those parts of the Ural region which formerly were counted as part of Asia.

[12] It is difficult to draw exact comparisons, as the administrative boundaries have changed several times. For instance, the Ural region comprises parts of Czarist Siberia, and so do the Soviet republics of Kazakstan and Kirgizistan. The autonomous regions of the Buriat-Mongols and of the Yakuts and the Far Eastern region lie wholly within the old Siberia. The last census was taken on January 17, 1939 (*The Statesman's Yearbook*, 1941).

[13] John Scott, *Behind the Urals* (Cambridge, Mass., 1942), p. 255, refers to new empty buildings erected in Magnitogorsk since 1939, whose pur-

industries, the lack of trained personnel, is thus avoided. (In exceptional cases, even in former times, whole industrial settlements with machinery, personnel, and even houses were moved.) [14] In the case of peasants moving to collective farms, the farm workers already at the place prepared houses — although often very primitive ones — for the expected newcomers. Delegates from Russia or the Ukraine visited places in different regions and finally chose one for their group. The choice seems to have been mostly influenced by similarities in economic conditions, in soil qualities, etc.[15] It became the normal thing to move whole factories according to the war conditions. Some plants went only to the Volga Valley, most to the Ural region — especially the Asiatic side — or to Western Siberia, and quite a few even farther east, or into Central Asia.

In addition to these transplanted industries possibly as many as 15 million evacuated people, particularly the skilled workers of these plants, party members, and Jews, moved to Asiatic Russia. Many of these people returned to their homes after the Germans were driven out of the occupied areas, but there are indications that not all will return.[15a] It is unlikely that the Soviets are returning many

---

pose remained a secret. So the capacity of the power stations was enlarged without any reason which was immediately recognizable.

[14] Such an example is given by Smolka, p. 133, where he discusses the town Nordvyk in the Katanga region in the Arctic. The transportation of prefabricated parts of houses was necessary in this treeless area. To the 150 pioneers, 600 other people were added in 1936, and their families were expected for the next year.

[15] See Anne Louise Strong, "Soviets behind the Ural," in *Asia*, October 1941, p. 545, and Georg Cleinow, *Neu Sibirien (Sib-Krai)* (Berlin, 1928), p. 238.

[15a] In "February, 1942 the Council of Peoples Commissaries issued an order requiring authorities in the eastern regions to make arrangements for the permanent absorption of workers and employees transferred there with their factories and equipment." Lorimer, p. 198.

plants to their former places. That does not mean that the old, well-located places will remain without industries. But they are being furnished with new equipment or machinery removed from Central Europe. There are good reasons for leaving the once-moved industries where they are besides the obvious disadvantage of interrupting production by dismantling and reinstallation. To be sure, the accommodations for these people suddenly brought to Asia are very bad, but the accommodations in Russia proper, devastated by the enemy and the scorched earth policy, will not be better. The strategic location is obviously better in Asia. As to the economic location, the same may be true, if estimates of Soviet experts are correct in any degree. According to these estimates, 85 per cent of the subterranean coal fields of the U.S.S.R. lie in Asia. The figures for copper, water power, wheatland, and iron ore are 87, 85, 60, and 28–40 per cent respectively.[16] In some cases the distance to the market may be greater; but this will be of small importance if the eastward movement of the population continues.

The Russians are moving into areas which were mostly sparsely settled before. Some parts of Siberia will probably continue to remain without any population worth mentioning, because of their climate; others had a relatively dense population in pre-Russian times. These are the irrigated river oases of Turkestan and the relatively small area between the Caucasus mountains and the Armenian highland. Most of Turkestan and the whole of Siberia were virtually empty spaces. Many of the regions into which the Russians moved had been depopulated by the devastating raids of the Manchus into Mongolia and Southern Siberia.

[16] *The New International Yearbook*, 1941.

Other territories had never known a large population, and were made available for a numerous population only through modern methods of irrigation, communication, mining, etc. Thus the Russians soon constituted the majority of the population in these areas without destruction of the natives, as the North American and Argentinian Indians had been destroyed. As early as 1700 there were more Russians in Siberia than natives.[17] Since then the number of natives has grown only slowly — a little by the addition of newly acquired territory, more by natural increase. Meanwhile the Russian immigration, and in a small degree the gradual assimilation of some tribes, had increased the number of Russians so rapidly that at the time of the First World War they comprised about 90 per cent of the total population. Some of the primitive tribes had decreased or even died out because of new diseases, such as measles, and the abuse of alcohol;[18] the new policy of the Soviets towards the nationalities is said to have brought about a new swift increase among these primitive tribes.[19] Still, at the present time and probably for some time in the future the higher birth rate among the Russians and the large immigration will tend to diminish further the percentage of natives. Moreover, in those communities whose isolation is broken, their rise to a higher level of civilization may promote intermarriage and Russification.

The trend to Russification in the Soviet state, despite official discouragement of such a policy, is unmistakable.

[17] Schultz, p. 167, gives statistics back to 1622, though the older ones with due reserve.

[18] Wladimir K. Arsenjew, *Russen und Chinesen in Ostsibirien* (Berlin, 1903), p. 24.

[19] Smolka, p. 23, cites the famous Russian explorer Otto Juliewitsch Schmidt as his source.

We have only little statistical mate███ ██ ce its working,
such as figures for intermarriage.[19a] ██ ██an safely assume
that in most mixed marriages one party was Russian and
more children were brought up in the Russian than in the
language of the other parent.

By moving into Soviet Asia most Russian peasants and
workers came into a predominantly Russian environment,
while people from Ukraina or Belorussia, moving into Siberia, had to communicate with their neighbors in Russian
even when they were numerous enough to retain their
national identity. The general result is clear and can be
confirmed by statistics. While the general increase of the
population of the Soviet Union from 1926 to 1939 was 16
per cent, that of the Russians was 27 per cent. Few nations
in the Soviet Union, mostly the small inconsequential ones,
have an equal or better record.[19b]

The Siberian, that is, the descendant of the Russian im-
migrant, has some distinctive features as compared with the
Russian of Europe. He is energetic, independent, self-
reliant, and has fewer moral and religious ties, although
there are religious communities which cling very strongly
to their particular denomination. Such groups, for example,
old-believers, "raskolniki," etc., were exiled to Siberia in the
time of the Czars and survived there. All these characteristics can be found with other colonial peoples, although not
all of them always at the same place or at the same time.

[19a] The percentage of mixed marriages increased from 1927 to 1937

in Ukraine	Armenia	Kazakhstan
7.5%	1 %	4.6%
19 %	7.4%	7 %

Bruno Plaetschke, *Sovietrussische Entwicklung als Gegenstand Geog-
raphischer Beobachtung und Darstellung.* — *Petermanns Mitteilungen*
(1941, vol. 87, Heft 2), p. 58.

[19b] Lorimer, p. 137.

The democratic tren among other colonial peoples is not completely lacking among the Siberians,[20] but is clearly recognizable only when they are compared with the Russians of the homeland, not with other colonials who have developed a genuine democracy. We see again a new nation in the making, Russian in core, but modified by the conditions of colonial life, modified also by the influx of foreign blood. Russian absorption of these Siberian tribes by intermarriage has not encountered great difficulties, since the Russians have been absorbing Finnish and Tatarian tribes uninterruptedly since the dawn of history.[21]

South of the Siberian border in Central Asia the Russians have been a minority up to the present day. The climate is less attractive, the few irrigated oases are fairly well populated, and the civilization of the inhabitants, who are mostly Mohammedan, is on a fairly high level. We can, therefore, not be so sure that the next development there will be similar to that of Siberia, though there are some indications of a parallel evolution. While the Russian immigration in the Czarist epoch was numerically insignificant, consisting of government officials, army personnel, some merchants, and only a few agricultural settlers, these few immigrants were strong enough, through their political and national consciousness, to keep Turkestan in the Union with Moscow during the civil war, in spite of the active nationalists, who were relatively few. The majority of the population were politically uninterested nomads and illiterate peasants.[22] Industrialization under the Soviets brought large masses of Russian speaking people into this region. The natural

[20] Cleinow, p. 128.

[21] Among Russians of world fame Artzibashev came from a family of Tatar descent; Lenin very probably had Tatar blood in his veins.

[22] Bosworth Goldman, "The New Aspect of the Central Asian Ques-

increase of the native population could hardly keep pace.[23] The Kazakhs even decreased considerably. Apparently this was because of excessive deaths during the years of collectivization and settlement of the nomads. Emigration, especially into Sinkiang, was also a factor.

The Bolshevist revolution affected Islam, although in a lesser degree than the Orthodox church. The spread of atheism has removed a very strong barrier against intermarriage and assimilation. The promotion of natives to leading posts has induced them to learn and use the Russian language without any compulsion. Although the Soviets favor the native languages, it is easily understandable that Russian should be used in professional work, for technical expressions, in administration, etc. The Soviets strictly deny any such purpose, but people who become members of the Communist party automatically become at the same moment members of a Russian-dominated society. Though the number of natives in the communistic organizations, especially in the youth organization, the *Komsomol*, is rapidly increasing, the number of Russians remains very strong.[24] The

---

tion," *Journal of the Royal Central Asian Society*, XX (1933), 369, mentioned on this occasion especially the retired Russian officials who remained in Turkestan after their retirement but continued to consider Moscow the only possible center.

[23] Strong, p. 547, says that in 1941 the number of Russians in Kazakstan was equal to the number of Kazaks. The same ratio concerning Tadzhikistan is reported by Rosita Forbes, *Forbidden Road, Kabul to Samarkand* (London, 1937).

[24] In 1925 there were in the *Komsomol*, the communist youth organization in Turkmenistan, 35 per cent Turkmen, but 56.7 per cent at the end of 1929. Almost the same numbers are given for the Kazaks in Kazakstan (34.7 per cent to 55.2 per cent). Among the adult members of the communist party, the Russians numbered at this time (Jan. 1, 1930) 44 per cent in Turkmenistan (the Turkmen 41 per cent), and 38 per cent in Kazakstan (43 per cent Kazaks). See Hans Kohn, *Nationalismus in der Sowjetunion* (Frankfurt a. M., 1932), p. 149.

Soviets win the youths of these Central Asian peoples first
for communism, secondly for a common future, third, in
our opinion, for assimilation. The promotion of the native
languages by the Soviets tends in its ultimate effect to make
Russification easier, removing from the native languages the
sting of inferiority and thus preventing an undesirable psychological reaction. A man who uses the Russian language
for practical and technical purposes will not be considered
a traitor.[25] What the Catholic faith did toward uniting
Christianized Indians and Spaniards into a more or less
homogeneous mestizo nation in many Latin-American countries the communist doctrine seems to be doing in Asia.
"The few natives who took part in the Turkestan revolution have become so Russified in outlook that they feel only
the Communist missionary urge." [26] The identification of
Russification with communism in this quotation is entirely
incidental. When groups of natives were united with
Russia in a class struggle against the "common enemy," this
enemy was first the Russian bureaucracy, which is liquidated today. The common enemy of the present moment
consists of the Mohammedan mullahs and the tribal chiefs.
Their final destruction may help toward the creation of a
united nation blended from different sources. So a new
"melting pot" is in progress, the product of which will be
determined mainly by the Russian inheritance.

The fewest indications that a new Russian-Asiatic people

[25] M. O. Tchokaieff, "Fifteen Years of Bolshevik Rule in Turkistan,"
Journal of the Royal Central Asian Society, XX (1933), 358, states that
the number of Kazak-kirghis diminished from 6,500,000 in 1917 to 5,000,000
in 1932. Giving ample allowance to a surplus of deaths over births and
strong exaggeration by this fanatically anti-Soviet nationalist writer, his
statement seems to indicate a definite trend to Russification. However,
his figures can not be brought into accord with the official census returns.

[26] Goldman, p. 370.

will arise are to be found in the Caucasus, although even here they are not lacking altogether. In the Caucasus the Russians do not constitute more than a fourth of the total population. Secluded mountain valleys favor separatism in language and manners. Furthermore, there has been no strong influx of war-refugee industries into this area, as far as we can judge from the news. On the other hand, the peoples of the Caucasus have given to Russia a number of leading men, among whom may be mentioned Stalin himself;[27] Tsheidse and Tshenkeli, the leaders of the former social democratic party; Karachan, an Armenian, the well-known Soviet diplomat. There are too many of these for them to be regarded only as individuals who have come more or less by chance into another people: as, for instance, the Corsican Napoleon came into France. Nobody will contend that France was influenced by Corsica through the isolated personality of Napoleon, nor do these leaders coming into Russia from the Caucasus represent the influence of their section. Their easy integration into Russian society and civilization certainly has been facilitated by the old civilization of the Caucasus region, by its similar social structure, and by the related Christian faith of Armenians, Georgians, etc. However, these people have gone into Russia and played their role there; the Caucasus area has not yet become a new center.

On the other hand, there was no Siberian among all the leading men of Czarist Russia. But many returned exiles, Lenin, Trotsky, and Stalin among them, knew Siberia and, consciously or not, were influenced by its potentialities. Furthermore we can point to movements in Siberia itself to secure for Siberia a proper position within the Rus-

[27] His original Georgian name is Djugashvili.

sian Empire. As early as 1863 a movement started aim-
ing at autonomous status for Siberia, and at the same
time a certain influence upon the central government
made itself felt. Similar movements which arose a little later
in Central Asia and the Caucasus were somewhat tinged
with the nationalism of the respective nationalities and
seemed to aim at autonomy only as a preparation for complete separation from Russia. But the desires of the Siberian
Cossacks and the peoples of Central Asia for autonomy
seemed so similar to the Czarist government that it declined
to construct a railroad between these two countries in spite
of the obvious and freely admitted economic advantages of
such a road.[28] After the revolution of 1905 there were in
the Duma, besides the anti-governmental delegates of all
non-Russian peoples, a similar oppositional group of Siberian autonomists. A few months later the government
through a *coup d'état* abolished the parliamentary representation of Central Asia, reduced the number of representatives from Siberia from 21 to 15, and reduced those from the
Caucasus from 29 to 10, dividing the latter delegation into
two groups, the one elected by Russians, the other by non-
Russians.

We shall skip Siberia's role during the revolutionary
period from 1917 to 1920, when the autonomy movement
headed a short-lived attempt to obtain full independence.
The Bolshevist policy of colonization, economic development, and favoring local autonomy made every dangerous
movement disappear. While no faction remained which
would advocate political separation, the influence of the
local authorities on the central authorities grew steadily.[29]

[28] Cleinow, p. 57.
[29] For an example see Cleinow, p. 73, on the role of the regional administration at Novosibirsk since 1924.

A foreign observer remarks: "The economic dependency of the Soviet Union on Western Siberia is growing. Siberia's sturdy peasantry is, therefore, likely to exert an increasing political influence on the general policy of the Union." [30] It is sometimes difficult to trace the origin of a particular measure to the "benevolent despotism" of the center or to the pressure of the local authorities. The fact itself can not be denied. There exists perhaps only one example from the former period. A group of adventurers and speculators in lumber living in the Far East were active in managing the war with Japan in 1904. Their uncontrolled but strongly backed policy contributed in leading Russia into that war. Today the influences radiating from Asia are much more continuous, although they do not influence the foreign as much as the economic policy. Jakuts, Buriats, and Kirghiz were able to secure for their regions the establishments of plants which were originally designed for other places. The wishes of Western Siberia, coinciding with the wishes of the leading strategists, secured the construction of a second railroad parallel to the older main line instead of the construction of a third track, which was recommended by the experts in the Moscow central offices.[31]

We have stated in a former chapter that the political union directed the influence of the Dominions mainly to Great Britain, while the United States, being an independent country, could influence countries all over the world. We should not be surprised to find in the isolated, mainly self-sufficient Soviet Union a similar impact of the Asiatic provinces on Russia proper alone. The outcome of World War II, especially on the Russian front, depended largely

[30] Goldman, p. 364.
[31] Cleinow, p. 313.

on the fact that Russian Asia was able to support the European part of the Soviet Union to a considerable degree.

Today a number of European nations are under Russian influence politically, economically, and ideologically. Russian books, magazines, and films are not only the almost exclusive foreign products in a number of East European countries, but circulate freely also in a number of other countries such as Austria, Italy, France, and the Scandinavian countries. Before World War II such influence was restricted to Asiatic countries, where it played an undeniable role. It may be difficult always to distinguish the influence coming from Moscow and the influence exerted from Asiatic places. It is undeniable that Turkey, Iran, and Afghanistan are impressed by the development in the Mohammedan parts of the Soviet Union, Mongolia is impressed by the development in the Buriato-Mongolic Soviet Republic, and from countries more distant the threads often do not lead to Moscow but to Central Asia or Eastern Siberia. Even Indian Socialists like Jawaharlal Nehru, though impressed by the Russian experiment in general, look for the real proof of its adaptability for India to its success in Central Asia.[32] Dzungaria and Sinkiang have the best outlet today through the Turksib railroad. The papers edited in Tashkent, not the Moscow press, are read in Chinese Turkestan. It was a troupe of actors and musicians from Tadzhikistan, not a troupe of Russians, who toured Afghanistan and Iran in 1941, preparing psychologi-

[32] Jawaharlal Nehru, *Toward Freedom* (New York, 1941; the American edition of his autobiography). He states on p. 229 that he was "impressed by the reports of the great progress made by the backward regions of Central Asia under the Soviet regime." On p. 286 he discusses the problem of the Latin script, not only in reference to its abstract merits, but also in reference to Turkish and Central Asian experience.

cally the path for the favorable reception of Russian troops several months later.[33] We may remember that American influence was felt in the Far East and in the Caribbean area much earlier than in Europe. We feel entitled to say that the center of balance has already begun to shift to the East, although the capital may remain indefinitely in Moscow, as the capital of the United States remained in Washington even when the South had long ceased to be the most important section of the United States. It seems clear, however, that Leningrad, which is too far from the Asiatic parts of the Soviet Union, will never recover her position as capital.

There is no doubt that we are observing here only the first stage of the shifting of the center of balance. It begins here, as in the United States, in the economic field. There are still only a few signs of a shifting of the cultural center. The flourishing universities in Omsk, Irkutsk, Tashkent, the valuable services in prospecting new treasures of the subsoil furnished by the Siberian branch of the Geographic Society of Irkutsk, together with the damage done by the present war to older sites of learning in the West, point in this direction. It may prove even more important that illiteracy is about to disappear entirely. Russia will never be able to treat the Asiatic population, Russian or not, as a group of colonials without any will of their own.[34]

There is, however, an important difference from the countries we have discussed hitherto. The migration to Asia and the shift of the center have taken place in contiguous areas. The Latin-American countries, the British

---

[33] Raymond A. Davies and Andrew J. Steiger, *Soviet Asia* (New York, 1942), p. 161.
[34] This factor is stressed particularly by Stéber, p. 237.

Dominions, the United States, all arose in countries separated from the European homelands by vast expanses of ocean. The absence of contiguity provided an intermediate period of isolation which we found everywhere, though not always so sharply marked as in South America. The new centers had an ample breathing space in which to develop their own nationality and their own civilization. This leads us to the question whether the Russian development really can be put into the same class with the development of these other countries. Before definitely claiming that it can, we should like to recall briefly two historical cases of shifting centers within contiguous areas.

Germany's *Drang nach dem Osten*, her longing for the East, pushed her borders from the Elbe and Saale into territory originally Slavic. This movement was directed first more to the southeast, later to the northeast. The political center followed. From the Rhine, where the political center was located in the period of the powerful medieval emperors, it shifted to Prague, Vienna, and at last to the Prussian Berlin. The economic center lagged behind. It shifted at no time so far eastward as to reach Vienna or any part of Austria. The Rhineland was never weakened economically so much as it was politically, although Berlin without doubt was the financial center of the Second and Third Reich. Today's indications are that the Ruhr will become the economic center for postwar German economy. Culturally, the ascendancy of Berlin over the older centers was even slower and scarcely a fact up to World War I. Since the First World War the leading publishing firms have moved their central offices from Leipzig and Stuttgart to Berlin and it became the country's dramatic center. The effect of World War II is harder to determine in the cultural field than in those concerning other human activities.

Perhaps even more instructive is the American parallel, where the demographic and economic center had the lead and was followed by the political centers. The Revolution not only freed the thirteen original colonies, but also opened the way for the small farmers of the backwoods to assert their ascendancy over the big harbor towns on the seaboard. The capital of Georgia moved from Savannah over several stations to Atlanta, and the capitals of South Carolina, North Carolina, Virginia, Pennsylvania, New Jersey, New York, and New Hampshire also moved further inland. At the new sites they remained fixed, although later Philadelphia and New York City, at least, attained a much higher importance than the areas represented by Harrisburg and Albany respectively. The epoch of capitalistic industrialism has again enhanced the importance of the Northeast in general. Nevertheless, the westward movement is the most characteristic feature of American history until the disappearance of the "last frontier" at the end of the nineteenth century.[35] We can even recognize an absolute loss of importance of the eastern centers, with the possible exception of New York. The agriculture of New England is definitely decaying. Some of the old industries of the eastern seaboard have shifted to new locations farther west or south, such as textile industries since the thirties. The rapid development of shipyards and war industries on the West Coast and in the South was along previously established lines. Quite a few, though not all, of the plants and many workers came to stay. Another characteristic instance is

[35] Frederick Jackson Turner, *The Frontier in American History* (New York, 1920).

the rise of shipyards constructing seagoing vessels on the Great Lakes. As early as 1910 the census return showed that of the states whose industrial output represented the highest value the majority were situated in the Middle West.[36]

Although the continuous area favored the gradual shift of centers of population, industry, and civilization, the very history of the United States proves that this is no essential difference as compared with the development of overseas centers. There was a period in the history of the United States when the West seemed to break away from the East, as the thirteen colonies had broken away from England a few decades earlier. When the pioneers crossed the Appalachian range, their needs in the new country were too different from those of the older colonies to guarantee them an appropriate administration. Besides, the means of transportation were too slow to vouchsafe the efficiency of the very best government as long as it was located in the older centers. The moral strength and the self-consciousness of the frontier folk were too strong to let their wishes be neglected. On the other hand, they were too few, their settlements too far away and isolated, to be able to dominate the older settlements. For a short time it seemed as if these settlers would secede from the United States. But finally North Carolina and Virginia renounced their claims to the western territories, and Kentucky and Tennessee joined the older states as equals.

The Russian analogy is striking. The organization of a

[36] The census taken between 1935 and 1940 valued the industrial output of the following states above one billion dollars: New York, Illinois, Michigan, Pennsylvania, Ohio, New Jersey, California, Massachusetts, Indiana, Wisconsin, Texas, North Carolina, Missouri.

federative Soviet Union opens the path for the emergence of new political centers, following the shift of centers of population and economy. The short-lived independent Siberia of 1919 is a strange analogy to those Tennessean and Kentuckian settlements which considered secession necessary in the 'nineties of the eighteenth century. Thirty years later the same Tennessee gave to the Union that typical frontier democrat Andrew Jackson as president. During the nineteenth century he had thirteen followers in the presidential chair, of whom only four were not connected with the West either by birth or by residence.[37]

The shrinking distances and the decreasing importance of geographic obstacles helped to avoid a break within the United States as they help today to keep together the Dominions and the United Kingdom as well as the different parts of the Soviet Union. The Appalachians were certainly a greater obstacle at the time of Washington than the Urals, the steppes of the Kirghiz, and the Caucasus are today.

This mechanical view, however, is not sufficient. It is certain that some of Great Britain's statesmen had learned the lesson of the American Revolution when they granted self-government to Canada. So had the American statesmen who inaugurated the policy of equality of rights in the organization of new states in the newly acquired territories. So had the Bolshevists when they profited from these successful experiments in federalization, as well as from the

[37] Charles A. and Mary R. Beard, *The Rise of American Civilization* (New York, 1927), I, 508. Hoover was the first president from west of the Mississippi, but the vice-presidents since 1933 have all come from west of the Mississippi: Charles Curtis from Kansas, John N. Garner from Texas, and Henry A. Wallace from Iowa. Harry S. Truman came from Missouri and moved from the vice-presidency to the presidential chair.

disasters of European nationalist struggles, although the originality of their federalist scheme in many aspects is undeniable.

There is, indeed, one factor which puts the Russian development in line with the development of the overseas countries, rather than with that in contiguous territories such as in Germany or the United States: the European partner in the Soviet Union is absolutely declining through being involved in the general European catastrophe.

CHAPTER VI

The Small Nations

WHEN COLUMBUS set sail for America, the population of Europe, however inhomogeneous in itself, was fairly distinct from the population of other continents.[1] The descendants of this European population are the bearers of Western civilization. At least one fourth of them live outside Europe today,[2] and the overwhelming majority of them live within the territories we have discussed in previous chapters. Our thesis, as we have stated it before, is valid only if one concedes that there is not only a shifting of centers of these foremost colonizing nations, but that all

[1] Only a very few individuals belonging to these peoples were to be found in Asiatic or African areas; there were some in Palestine and in the Greek fringe of Asia Minor. The eastern boundary of the Greek Orthodox faith in Russia may be considered the line of demarcation between Asia and Europe in these parts of the twin continents at this moment. We might as well fix this line arbitrarily because geographers have never succeeded in reaching an agreement about its proper position. The invading Turks in the Balkan Peninsula were clearly foreigners to Europe; they had not yet acquired customary acceptance as Europeans. Furthermore, they were Mohammedans, as were the Tatars in Southern and Eastern Russia, whom we have excluded from definition as Europeans. There were some heathen tribes in Northern and Northeastern Europe — Lapps, Samoyedes, etc. — but they are of no concern whatsoever for our investigation. At the time mentioned the main bulk of Christians lived in Europe, with the exception of some sects of distinctly oriental character such as Abyssinian Christians, Nestorians, etc. There were hardly any converts to Catholicism among Negroes and Chinese.

[2] Alexander Carr-Saunders, "Europe Overseas," in Julian S. Huxley's *We Europeans*, p. 241n., puts the number of Europeans in Europe at 476,000,000, and of people of European descent overseas at 164,000,000; both figures are for 1929.

Europeans are involved. Though we have stressed the fact that the influence of the new centers beyond the sea is not confined to their mother countries but exerted in varying degrees on all European nations, it may help clarify our point to review briefly all the other European nations, whether they possess colonies or whether they seem confined to Europe on a political or linguistic map.

We have already discussed the Irish influence in the United States, through the United States, and from the United States upon Great Britain and Ireland.[3] Though their number is widely disputed, there is no doubt that more Irishmen live in the United States and in the British Dominions than in Eire. Though Ireland has somewhat recovered her position not only as the emotional, but also the intellectual, Irish center, the influence of the Irish-American center is much more diversified and stronger. The question of an independent Irish state in America can never arise, since there is no extended area of contiguous Irish settlements. The influence of the Irish Free State is not only limited by its small size and its small population, by its remoteness from the main lifelines of Europe as well as intercontinental economic and intellectual traffic, but also by its self-imposed seclusion through the adoption of the old Gaelic language, which can not become familiar to the main bulk of overseas Irish. Even under the most favorable conditions, English must remain the language of daily intercourse for the overseas Irish. They will have the instrument with which to influence others, the European Irish as well as Americans and British at large, while an Irish Free State center at the best can only influence a part of the overseas Irish. It is significant that the two Nobel prize

[3] Cf. Chapter III, pp. 90–91.

winners of Irish descent, George Bernard Shaw and Eugene
O'Neill, write only English, the former living in England,
the latter in the United States.

One may wonder whether this Irish center in the United
States is a transitory phenomenon, bound to disappear with
the complete assimilation of the Irish into the English-
speaking American environment. This may be, as is suggested by the advanced integration of the Irish in some sections; in others, however, they have kept rather apart from
the main bulk of Americans and continue to form a clearly
distinguishable community whose distinct existence is
stressed and somewhat secured by the Roman Catholic
faith.

It would be too narrow a definition to consider only
national and political bodies as centers of Western civilization. Among other cultural units churches are of particular
significance, and we shall therefore turn aside to discuss
them at this point. With regard to the Protestant churches
we can be very brief, since this question with relation to the
Protestant denominations in the United States was dealt
with in Chapter IV.[4] The tendency of these denominations
to split invites the foundation of new organizations in newly
settled countries and weakens the mutual influence considerably. Although referring to a country outside the plan
of our study, the following statement on the Protestant
church in China is revealing: "The indigenous Chinese
Church . . . is today a reality . . . in many centers no
longer finds its greatest resources either of personnel or of
funds in the missions. . . . The mission in China aims to
merge itself in a Chinese Church, which is free to develop
its own life and organization without being linked denomi-

[4] Cf. Chapter IV, p. 114.

nationally to any branch of the Churches in the West." [5]
The situation in the Protestant independent churches in less
exotic countries is intrinsically the same.

The situation of the Roman Catholic Church is completely different. There are analogies, as, for example, in
the Irish branch. The first priests came from Ireland to
tend the American flock. Today the seminaries in the
United States educate enough young priests for the American churches and occasionally even send priests to Ireland
herself.[5a] There are Roman Catholic churches attended predominantly by Irish, French-Canadian, and Polish Catholics, etc., and also in charge of priests of the same origin.
Nevertheless, the organization of parts of the Catholic
Church in national units seems rather accidental. The unity
of the Roman Catholic Church is not endangered by such
administrative devices, nor is its hierarchic body affected
by such national divisions. Moreover, the hierarchic organization of the Roman Catholic Church as a unit seems unfit
to shift its center. The Holy See in Rome is the unchange-
able center, and its influence may extend or shrink, but in
principle never shifts. Even here, however, there are some
small indications of influences from secondary centers.
Once in a long time, when a new Pope is elected, cardinals
may influence the attitude of the Church for the coming
term. The number of non-European cardinals in the
Sacred College has been increased from 5 to 21, and now
includes 14 from South America and one Chinese. Modern
means of communication enable them to attend the con-
clave. In 1947 the 400-year-old order of the Vincentians

[5] *China Christian Year Book*, 1936–37, pp. 191, 195.
[5a] Some non-European countries, though long Roman-Catholic, still
have to draw on European-trained and European-born priests. This is
true of Brazil.

for the first time failed to choose a French Superior General, selecting instead an American. There are bishops and archbishops who are Chinese, Indians, or Negroes.[6] True, this is only a faint symptom. There are slight indications too that the Roman Catholic Church might share the fate of the Spanish Empire, if it did not allow some influence to the outlying parts. At the time of the severance of political ties with Spain Bishop Aglipay founded a new church in the Philippines, one which was essentially Catholic, but autonomous and national. It was said that it had 2 million members at a time. More recent are the attempts of Luis Castillo Mendez to read the Mass in Spanish and to found a Venezuelan Apostolic Church in 1947, and of the Bishop of Moura in 1946 to establish a Brazilian Apostolic Church in São Paolo. The very beginnings of a movement in America tending to modify the hierarchic dependencies into a structure more conformable with American republican and democratic ideas were crushed. Pope Leo XIII condemned this "false Americanism" in his Apostolic Letter of January 1899 to Archbishop Gibbon, *Testem Benevolentiae*. There is no sign that the failure of this movement weakened American Catholics' loyalty towards the papacy. On the other hand, about the same time the Knights of Columbus formed

[6] A Catholic hierarchy was established in China in 1875, in North Africa in 1884, in India in 1886, and in Japan in 1891. But not before 1926 were the first Chinese consecrated in Rome as bishops. In 1937 there were already 13 Chinese bishops and 10 Prefects Apostolic among 129 ecclesiastical areas. A majority of the clergy was already Chinese, 1835 among 4452 priests, 689 brothers (55 per cent of the total), and 3626 sisters (63 per cent of the total). Among the missionaries there were 8000 European priests and 6000 native priests. The Protestants even earlier appointed Chinese as presidents of colleges, etc. Among them the number of native missionaries (5000) almost equals the number of Europeans and Americans (5700). These figures are given by Hayes, pp. 150–151, and *China Year Book*, pp. 114, 122.

a powerful organization of laymen within the Catholic Church. A leading American historian considers it "no accident that the leading Catholic laymen's organization in the world was founded" in America.[7]

We need mention only briefly the Greek Orthodox Church. This church, although dogmatically united like the Roman Catholic Church, is divided into national churches. If its formerly strongest branch, the Russian Church, should recover at all, it will certainly share the geographic and demographic fate of the Russian people.

Among the religions of Europe the weakest numerically was the Jewish. The European center of Jewry is definitely destroyed. Before 1880 more than 90 per cent of all Jews lived in Europe. The Russian pogroms drove hundreds of thousands over the ocean. New communities were established, the most important ones in Palestine and the United States. The First World War destroyed the economic preponderance of European Jewry; the atheistic Bolshevist revolution destroyed many of their centers of religious learning. Palestine and the United States became new intellectual, economic, and religious centers. The stream of migrants from the old to the new centers continued. The Bolshevists tried to lead the Jews from their western provinces into Asia, for many years with only small success. The Jewish center in Poland remained the strongest numerically and spiritually until the present war. This present war precipitated all the aforesaid movements. Today, outside the British Isles, there is hardly one of the European Jewish centers left undamaged. Schools, synagogues, foundations, property, have been destroyed, and the population driven out, decimated,

[7] C. A. and M. R. Beard, *The Rise of American Civilization*, II, 749.

physically almost annihilated. What is left in German-dominated Europe is an impoverished mass, almost without children, counting hardly more than a fourth of total Jewry. On the other hand, the Jewish centers in the United States and Palestine have been strengthened, if not economically, at least numerically, and perhaps spiritually. At least we see that American-born social workers and rabbis and Palestine-trained teachers had to rebuild Jewish life in some almost destroyed Central European communities. And even in Russia a shifting to Asia has taken place. Since the majority of the Russian Jews lived in the western provinces, a larger percentage of Jews than of Russians was transplanted to Asia with the movement from those provinces eastward. The discussion of the Jewish problem has led us back from our discussion of churches to the fate of the small nations, since in the case of the Jews religious organization and nation very nearly coincide.

The Germans prepared a similar fate for other European nations, first of all the Czechs, Poles, Slovenes. Their cultural institutions, in some cases down to the elementary schools, were closed; their educated classes threatened with extinction. Germanization or destruction, in any case their slower or swifter disappearance from the European map as individual nations, was not far off. During this trying period secondary centers of these nations outside their original territory, centers in the United States and also in Russia, won importance for survival far above that engendered by their numerical strength. It may be doubtful whether they could have perpetuated the life of these nations as cultural units integrated into and yet distinct from the English, Spanish, and Russian speaking majority. But if only a small but compact number could have escaped to be assimilated, the remainder would have sufficed to maintain a distinct cultural center. The history of such old bodies of emigrants as the Pennsylvania Dutch, the Germans of the Volga, etc., shows that such a balance is possible to obtain. Here we are not considering the political exiles who always dream of return, but whose sons, estranged from their homeland and unable to understand the patriotism of their fathers, are easily assimilated. We are considering only the compact colonies of immigrants who in the second and third generation still use the language of their ancestors. The story has still to be written of how much the Czech colonies from Texas to Iowa, the Slovenes of Pennsylvania and Ohio, the Poles, Serbs, etc. in Russia influenced the reconstruction and aided the recovery of their homelands. They to a high degree enabled the escaped leaders to carry on as representatives of their nations. Beneš and Masaryk came back with a wide experience not only of America and England, but also of the Czecho-American and English centers. The same is true for the exiles returning from Russia, for men such as Bierut, or even Tito, probably Dimitrow also. It seems hardly possible but that the new centers will become very influential in shaping the future of their European co-nationals.[8] The Polish, Serb, Czech, and Lithuanian communities in America feel responsible for maintaining the democratic reputation of their submerged nations. In return their self-reliance will be strengthened, the knowledge of their importance will grow. Thus the chance of their survival as distinct cultural centers will increase.

[8] Characteristic of the spreading notion of these changing relations are the writings of Louis Adamic, himself a Slovene, especially his *Two Way Passage* (New York, 1941). He stresses the task involved rather than the completed fact.

Rather than attempting to depict this development for all these small nations separately, we shall choose as an example the development of the Slovak nation, especially to the end of World War I. The small Slovak people sent a relatively numerous group to America. Here they became the "rich American uncles and cousins." The more primitive a society is, the stronger the influence of the successful and rich tends to be. Most of these people were thrifty and saved sums which, while not too conspicuous in the United States, were quite a fortune in peasant, backward Slovakia. Many returned with their savings; others settled permanently in the United States. It is difficult to state exactly the degree of education of the people returning home to Slovakia, but in a period when — before the First World War — the Hungarian government established schools which used the Magyar language exclusively, the great majority of the peasants remained virtually illiterate. Therefore those returning from America, though their schooling was perhaps far below the average standard of American education, formed an advanced element among their conationals. Under the rule of the Magyars, the few sons of Slovakian peasants who succeeded in passing through the higher schools, by means of this education in a foreign language and separation from any contact with Slav achievements, became thoroughly assimilated and strove to be acknowledged by the Magyars as members of the ruling society. It is no wonder that the Slovaks had no political leaders until relatively late. Now the migrants from America brought methods of conducting political struggles, and they often became the leaders of the local opposition. They occasionally read English newspapers, listened later to the English-speaking radio, and kept up a slight contact with an advancing world.⁹ America, especially Western Pennsylvania, became the cultural center for the Slovaks. Thus it is not surprising that the political question of the fate of Slovakia after the breakdown of the Magyar rule in 1918 was virtually decided by the Slovaks of Pittsburgh and by their agreement with the Czech leader Masaryk, himself a Slovak.

There are other nations in Europe whose centers seem to be founded fairly safely on European soil, even in view of the present world situation. But on more thorough scrutiny indications of a shift can be discovered almost everywhere. The Scandinavian countries have so high a degree of civilization that it seems improbable that they can be influenced by American emigration centers, but the poverty of their soil and the adversity of climatic conditions threatens them with the fate of Ireland. Norway and Iceland have already sent almost one-third of their population overseas, and the percentage of Swedish and Danish emigrants is only a little smaller.¹⁰ How far this interrelation goes, unnoticed though it is in its wider implication, chance remarks by authors interested in different things may show, such as the following: "Not long

⁹ Oscar Jaszi, *The Dissolution of the Hapsburg Monarchy* (Chicago, 1929), p. 393, tells how court-room proceedings in pre-war Hungary revealed the fact that pan-Slavic and religious propaganda among the Ruthenians was not carried on from near-by Russia, but by Ruthenians emigrated to the United States.

¹⁰ The available figures are defective, but sufficient to justify the statement given in the text. For instance, the Canadian census gives the number of Icelanders in Canada as 19,382. Adding the similar number of Icelanders in the United States, the sum is equal to about one-third of the 108,000 inhabitants of Iceland proper in 1930. There were 93,000 Norwegians in Canada, and 348,000 foreign born and 752,000 of foreign or mixed parentage in the United States. There are several thousands more in the Dominions and South America, together more than 40 per cent of the population of Norway (2,800,000).

after Johan Bojer wrote *Emigrants* telling of those who set out bravely to make new homes in America, an answer seemed to echo from our own Middle West, as O. Rölvaag in *Giants in the Earth* described both happiness and hardships among the homesteaders in the Dakotas." [10a] Denmark has even developed a colony in Greenland. The climatic conditions in that outpost, however, allow only a very small population to live there, hence it is hardly to be assumed that a Danish overseas center will develop there. The strongest influence upon the European Danish center comes from the United States and Canada, from the Danish centers specifically as well as from the great influence exerted by the American and Canadian centers generally. The political colonial connection is of no avail. The same is true for the present Spanish colonial empire. We have had no reason whatsoever to mention these Spanish colonies when we have discussed the emergence of new Spanish-speaking centers.

A little more important for the mother country are the remaining Portuguese colonies. Portugal neglected her empire for nearly a century after the loss of Brazil. After the overthrow of the monarchy in 1910 she granted deliberating councils to her colonies and several seats in the Lisbon parliament. Although these concessions were made for the purpose of securing the adherence of the colonies and as a natural consequence of the newly adopted liberal theories, they opened the way for the population of the colonies to influence the old center. The number of people in the colonies to whom this opportunity was given is best circumscribed by the extent of the suffrage. All people having any Portuguese blood in their veins are considered

[10a] Alma Luise Olson, *Scandinavia* (1940), p. 227.

Portuguese and enfranchised, and in addition, all well-educated natives. On the basis of the common Roman Catholic faith and of a Portuguese school tradition, new peoples seemed to emerge in the different colonies, Portuguese in their language and tradition, but only partly so in their descent. The establishment of a dictatorship has destroyed the possibility of recognizing either the progress or the standstill of such a development by scrutinizing institutional evolutions. The news from the colonies which reaches the outside world, interested in entirely different problems, is too sparse to allow us to form any judgment.

There is one aspect, however, of this Portuguese development which must be discussed in more detail. The European center of civilization seemed to be willing to be influenced by overseas centers with a population of non-European stock but of related civilization. We have not envisaged this problem so sharply before, although we touched it in discussing the Latin-American and the Soviet Asiatic nations.

To these examples may be added the Maoris of New Zealand. They are of interest as the only colored race which has won virtually equal treatment with people of British descent. Today they share the cultural level of New Zealand's other citizens,[11] use the English language extensively, and have intermarried with the British immigrants so frequently that people of pure Maori blood are likely to vanish in the near future. Thus they have contributed to the formation of a future homogeneous population of New

[11] Cf. *A Dictionary of New Zealand Biography*, edited by G. H. Scholefield (Wellington, 1940), which proffers striking examples of how far the symbiosis has been carried on.

Zealand, modifying New Zealand's reaction upon the mother country.

There are other instances within the British Empire where colored people have not only contributed to but even constituted new centers of Western civilization of minor importance. The most important example is Jamaica. The attempt at self-government by the white inhabitants alone broke down in the middle of the nineteenth century, when cane sugar ceased to be the basis for immense wealth. This sugar crisis deprived the ruling white minority, the planter aristocracy, of their economic basis. After a period of crown-colony government by officials appointed from London, a new constitution was granted which enfranchised the colored people. The number of whites is rapidly de-clining.[12] On the other hand, the colored people have lost all knowledge of any African language. Since they have been enfranchised, "Jamaica is becoming an organic com-munity with a deep interest in its present and future and a perfectly natural pride in its position as a member of the British Commonwealth." [13]

Jamaica and the other West Indian islands are too small to rival the big centers, but they show the possibilities which may be in store for the British West African col-onies. These colonies harbor only a very few whites, mostly officials and merchants who return to Europe after some years of residence. Although there is no legal color bar, very seldom does an Englishman marry a native woman. Nevertheless, there is a certain education of the natives in

[12] In 1920 only 14,500 among 858,000. In 1941 the population was esti-mated at more than 1,223,000, the increase probably confined to the colored and black sections.

[13] *The Colonial Problem, A Report of a Study Group of Members of the Royal Institute of International Affairs* (London, 1937), p. 3.

European standards, connected with the spread of the English language. In Nigeria, the largest of these colonies, Negroes have taken over nearly all the functions which only two decades ago none but trained Europeans had been able to perform. The railways are run completely by native personnel.[14] Only a few European supervisors are left to guarantee the honesty of the employed. Even in the technical topographic service, which certainly needs high technical skill, Europeans have been replaced by natives. There is a college for natives which provides higher education for a restricted, but increasing, number. It is the Prince of Wales College at Ashimota, Gold Coast.[15] These English-speaking, educated natives are the spokesmen of the embryonic center. They attain a few influential positions, publish newspapers, form organizations such as the National Congress of British West Africa or the Gold Coast Aborigines Rights Protection Society. Thus a public opinion is formed which may even exert pressure on the administration. The governors are, indeed, empowered to use their own judgment as the only guide to their behavior in every respect; they are responsible in a general way to the Secretary for the Colonies in London. But since the voice of the natives can be heard in London and since it acts through favorably inclined members of Parliament, the influence of these colonies upon the British Government is an estab-

[14] The same is also true in the Belgian Congo, where the railroads are run entirely by natives. The economic world crisis helped here to bring about the same result because the government was forced to reduce the number of highly paid white employees. The number of whites in the Belgian Congo was reduced from 25,000 in 1930 to 20,000 in 1933. It increased, however, during the next years, attaining 27,791 on the census of Jan. 1, 1941.

[15] In 1915 a South African Native College was founded whose students are admitted as external candidates for the examinations at the University of South Africa.

lished matter, however weak it may be. They are centers
having characteristic features which fit exactly into the
general trend. They are, therefore, much more important
in principle — much more significant for our discussion —
than the culturally more highly developed British colonies
in East and Central Africa — Kenya, Northern and Southern Rhodesia. In these countries whites are not numerous
enough to impress their character upon the whole country
as in the Union of South Africa, but they are too numerous
to be of no avail as in West Africa.[16] The social, though
not legal, color bar permits the establishment of a small
center of Western civilization whose future is very precarious. The color bar also hinders the development of a
center of Western civilization constituted by natives because it keeps the natives from developing certain functions
indispensable for such a society. No prediction is involved
in this discussion whether these African countries will remain, or for how long, within a European-dominated
empire. But lacking a strong tradition of their own they
may be expected to develop a civilization of a European
type, whatever peculiarities it may show.

We should, indeed, be cautious in predicting the probable evolution of centers of Western civilization in all parts
of British West Africa. Northern Nigeria, especially, includes several petty Mohammedan kingdoms from which a
very efficient propagation of the Islamic faith is carried on
among the heathen tribes. These Mohammedan communities are in principle no bearers of Western civilization.
Though Western civilization may influence them, they are
essentially different. We meet here for the first time during
our investigation the phenomenon of a cultural renaissance.

[16] See page 57.

Such a renaissance may be prompted by the impact of Western civilization; it may absorb parts of it; but it is a development completely different from the rise of new centers of Western civilization, which alone is the subject of this essay. We consider not only China, Japan, Turkey, Iran, and the Arab countries outside the scope of our study, but also India, Burma, and Ceylon. What we witness in all these countries is entirely different from the emergence of new centers in South America, the British Dominions, the United States, or the Soviet Union. It is a genuine renaissance of old civilizations. It is doubtful whether such simultaneous renaissance movements in such different countries could have arisen without the impulse from Europe. They constitute an important factor in ousting Europe from the center of world happenings and in thereby upsetting the European order. But they are in no sense part of the development we have chosen to study, an evolution *within* the Western civilization. From our point of view it is quite unimportant whether India will become independent or remain a Dominion within the British Commonwealth of Nations. It might be that in the latter case India would influence political decisions within this Commonwealth; it would not be able to influence the cultural development more efficiently than it would from the outside, or than China does, for instance.

These influences of old or reviving civilizations may play an increasing role in the future, as it is clear even for the most inexperienced eye in the political field. It will be necessary — but very difficult indeed — to distinguish the genuine contribution of these civilizations from contributions which are reflections of the modern western influence. Scarcely anyone will deny that Arabic influence in the period of the Crusades, Chinese in the rococo, and Indian on some nineteenth-century philosophies were genuine contributions of these civilizations. The influence of Gandhi's non-violence movement is an undeniable Indian contribution in our time. But on the other hand, there is hardly anything genuinely Japanese in the advances and suggestions which have come from European-trained bacteriologists of Japanese birth, nor anything specifically Chinese in the discoveries of prehistoric men made by Chinese anthropologists. Even a play such as Rabindranath Tagore's *Postman* is unthinkable as a product solely of his Indian background, where the living tradition of drama did not exist. His influence may even have been stronger in European than in Indian literary circles. Indian Islam has developed a missionary movement in the Ahmediya which itself is a product of Western impact on Islam.

Whatever the significance and importance of such facts they will not change the general character of these old civilizations as the mainsprings of the modern Chinese, Persian, Indian, and other civilizations. We would have been justified in bypassing these civilizations completely for our topic, were it not for France. France has organized her empire so rigidly and uniformly that the question of winning the Mohammedans of Northern Africa for French civilization may be vital for the fate of the whole empire.

In the abstract, one would expect conditions to be favorable for the creation of overseas centers of French civilization constituted by a majority of people of non-European descent. The French attitude in general is not affected by racial prejudice as is the Anglo-Saxon attitude. It is true that the French in practice give fewer opportunities to the natives in their colonies to supplant the whites than the

British give in India or West Africa, for example. The decisive factor, however, is that the French consider every native a real Frenchman if he goes through the French school, avails himself of the French language, and adopts the French manner of living. Troubled postwar conditions have forced some changes of policy upon the French. Before 1945 the native had to relinquish his status under the tribal laws or the law of the Koran for the status of a French citizen. There was no pressure on him to do so; the French offered the alternative of naturalization as a French citizen or the right to remain within tribal or Moslem jurisdiction but in tutelage. They felt that in the long run French civilization would prove attractive enough to achieve a final cultural and legal unity in the empire. All inhabitants would finally be equal members of a cultural unit, the French civilization, considering themselves members of the French nation. "We want to make all our African subjects regardless of their racial origins into a single people, who will accept our speech as their common language. This common relationship will gradually produce a unified will." [17]

There are two partly opposing facts. One is that Frenchmen have wholeheartedly accepted as equal black citizens who have complied with the conditions sketched above; the other fact is that they have showed great reserve in actually conferring naturalization.

As for the first statement, it is sufficient to recall that not only Negroes from the West Indies and the Senegal regularly have had seats in the Paris parliament, but that a Negro from Martinique had a seat in a French cabinet.

[17] Quoted by Herbert Ingram Priestley, *France Overseas, A Study in Modern Imperialism* (New York–London, 1938).

There were fourteen deputies and senators in the French parliament from Africa, Indo-China, and the West Indies, most of them men of non-European stock. Only the representatives of the three North Algerian departments were mostly French. Since the end of the war the French have had to admit the Moslems of Algeria to political rights without requiring abandonment of their status as Moslems. The number of non-European overseas delegates in the French Parliament has increased considerably, not the least by the addition of these Moslems from Algeria. But the social attitude has not changed appreciably and the French in general have not lost their prewar attitude towards racial equality. This equality was not only official policy, but was apparent to every visitor to a Paris or Marseille coffee-house watching the behavior of the population, which showed no prejudice. I know of two physicians in a small village in Northern France, one of them a Russian emigrant, the other a Negro from the Senegal, both French citizens. There was no native French physician in the place. In the colonies, very often French officers and officials had a less cordial attitude. They were sometimes influenced by the attitude of Englishmen or Americans, but as often their attitude was caused mainly by their feeling of belonging to a higher social level which merely coincided with a racial difference.

On the other hand, it must be stressed that the number of such naturalized French citizens is relatively small. In some colonies, for example Madagascar, the practice of granting naturalization has become a little more liberal during very recent years. In theory the French native policy is much more liberal than the British; in practice the British are much more willing to give clerkships, etc., to natives. Among tribes of a low cultural level this British policy is quite successful, while among a population conscious of a civilization of its own the British attitude of social — not legal — discrimination and theoretical superiority has created much ill feeling. The French social affability and theoretical readiness to grant privileges — though often only in theory — has proved to be more efficient by its psychological implications. However, the tempo of admitting non-naturalized natives to a status of equality with French citizens has become faster during the last years. The franchise for local government has been extended to a growing number of colonies.[18] All inequalities and privileges in the matter of taxation were abolished first in Algeria, later in other colonies.

In French statistics the number of French and assimilated is given under a common heading. This is significant for the French attitude, but it leaves us without means of knowing exactly how far the French policy has succeeded. We know, however, that it failed completely among the Mohammedans of North Africa, with the exception of some tribes of Kabyles. Among the Kabyles there are villages where only French is spoken.[19] For the heathen or newly Christianized Negro of French West or Equatorial Africa, French citizenship was a privilege, and the abandonment of

[18] Algeria, Réunion, Martinique, and Guadeloupe were represented in both houses of the French Legislature; French India, Senegal, Guiana, and Cochin China in the Chamber of Deputies before World War II. Today only the two protectorates Morocco and Tunisia stand outside.

[19] Michael Pym, "The Franco-Muslim Position," *Journal of the Royal Central Asian Society*, XX (1933), 616. G. H. Bousquet, *A French View of the Netherlands Indies* (English translation, London–New York, 1940), p. 112, cites as an example the fact that there was a Kabyl leader of the French ultra-nationalistic organization "Croix de Feu" in the town Sidi Ouzan.

his tribal jurisdiction was no sacrifice at a period when tribal organization was breaking down anyway under the impact of modern economy.[20] The Jew of the North African ghetto has likewise reached a higher standing by accepting French jurisdiction, and at the same time he was able to remain a devoted member of his religious community. But the Islamic religious and civil laws are so interwoven in the Koran that a Mohammedan can not embrace French jurisdiction without endangering his religious status. As the Mohammedans represent the strongest and culturally most advanced element in the French colonies, assimilation is still rather slow. Furthermore, the emigration of French to the colonies has not yet furnished the necessary strong stock. There are indications that the French in Algeria have a higher birth rate than the French in France. But again the ambiguous classification of the French census makes it doubtful whether the increased birth rate is ascribable to genuine French families or naturalized Italians and Spaniards who may or may not become assimilated. There are British observers who consider that "an Algerian people [is] obviously forming itself, and it is becoming purposeless as well as almost impossible to distinguish French born from naturalized citizens." [21]

Also French authors recognize that this new Algerian population of European stock is not simply French.[21a] Probably the fusion of French, Spaniards, Italians and

[20] There were whole Senegalese villages which had French citizenship; whose young men were, therefore, free from forced labor, were not sent to France for military training, and had standing in French law courts (Priestley, p. 413).
[21] *Encyclopaedia Britannica* (14th ed., 1938), I, 615.
[21a] Henri Mausset, *France et Afrique du Nord* (Paris, 1945), p. 40: "C'est un nouveau peuple français qui se forme sur la terre algérienne...."

Maltese is less important than the contact with native civilization and the different conditions of life. As the American farmer is no longer a European peasant, so the Algerian *colon* is no longer simply French. He is more enterprising, imaginative, and adventurous, and has more fighting spirit.[21b] Nevertheless, the neo-French group remains a minority and its situation would be precarious if the program of final assimilation should miscarry. Even the influx of half a million French as refugees during the War has not changed the picture as most of these refugees probably returned to metropolitan France.

The stay of these refugees was too short, their contact with colonial life too precarious for them to be regarded as bearers of a colonial spirit to the homeland. There are, however, some signs that the colonial empire is going to influence France. For example, French painting is influenced strongly by the North African scene and in some ways by other colonies also. It was possible to regard Gauguin, Picasso, and Rousseau as single phenomena, but powerful personalities like these do not remain isolated. The increasing number of relatively unknown painters is a sure sign of a definitely established influence. More important is the fact that in French economy the weight of the North African colonies is making itself felt in matters which are not typical of colonial economy. Not long ago Algeria and Tunisia were known primarily as exporters of agricultural products. The beginning of the twentieth century added mining products, phosphates, and iron ores. After the First World War, industry began to settle down near the iron mines. It is a striking coincidence that the present war has not only driven Russian industry to Asia,

[21b] Mausset, p. 41.

but also French industry to Africa. It was no evacuation before the advancing foe, but a late move when France herself was starved of raw materials which were plentiful in North Africa but could not be transported. Factories for textiles and leather products, especially, moved. The finality and extent of these movements is not yet clear.

In cultural matters, however, France and even Paris have remained the center of French civilization, despite some small signs of a coming shift.[21c] This is one of the reasons why De Gaulle's attempt to establish a new center for the French empire in the colonies failed. Some of the necessary conditions were lacking. The Senegalese soldiers, the strongest and most reliable force in the colonial army, remained loyal to the government which sat at or at least near the old center; they were too primitive to recognize the threat to themselves, to their ascent to equality, which lay in the partial adoption of the Nazi racial principles. Most of them probably never have heard about Hitler's attitude toward the negroid "subhuman" races. De Gaulle was consistent with the old French policy in appointing a Negro governor general of Equatorial Africa. But it seems that the effect of this gesture was very weak. And it is significant that Felix Eboué was not an African Negro, but a native of Guiana, the French colony in South America.[21d]

Mohammedans in North Africa were somewhat aware of the danger which threatened them through the racial dogma, but they were not so well disposed toward the French rule as to furnish any basis for a self-reliant over-

[21c] Stéphane Lauzanne's *Retreat to the Empire*, quoted by Charles Antoine Micaud in *The French Right and Nazi Germany*, 1933–1939 (Durham, 1943), p. 19, said as early as 1939: "France has two capitals: Paris and Algiers."
[21d] He died May 17, 1944.

seas French empire. Finally, there is no great French colony where the French, even according to the legalistic interpretation, form the majority.[22]

There exists, however, such a country outside the French empire; the French Canadian province of Quebec. The French Canadians are a distinctive people, rather more so than English Canadians or Australians, hardly less than Americans, Peruvians, or Mexicans. It is true that French Canadian poets and writers look for recognition to Paris. But in all vital matters the development has been along other lines. French Canadians have been called Frenchmen untouched by Gallicanism, Enlightenment, Revolution.[23] Their civil law is based on the pre-revolutionary Coutume de Paris. They produce large families, strong enough to counterbalance the growth of the English-speaking part of the Canadian population although the latter is aided by immigration.[24] Their sympathies for Britain have changed with British policy, alternating between heartily offered loyalty and a rather suspicious attitude; their attitude toward France has remained suspicious, to say the least, since the French Revolution. Cultural influences from outside have been rather weak, barred by Church influence from Protestant England as well as from atheistic France. It has been said that expressions for modern things or

[22] In Algeria the "Europeans and assimilates" constituted a little more than 14 per cent of the population; in Oceania, 12¾ per cent. Even in small colonies, where this census interpretation shows a possible French majority, a closer investigation reveals the fallacy. Of the 190,000 "Europeans and assimilates" of Réunion, most are Negroes from East Africa (R. Kuczynski, *Population Movements*, Oxford, 1936, p. 99).

[23] McCormac, *Canada; America's Problem*, p. 167.

[24] The French Canadians increased from 65,000 in 1763 to 3,000,000 in 1931, without additional immigration. At certain periods there was even a strong emigration into the United States.

thoughts have sneaked into the French Canadian language rather from American colloquial English than from Oxford English or from European French.[25]

To sum up, we find in Quebec a situation analogous to the situation in Latin-American countries. A new center is developing and growing in numbers as well as in economic and cultural weight, equal in importance at least to the many cultural centers of small nations in Europe. It is one more of these overseas centers to which the balance is shifting. Quebec and Montreal, like Rio de Janeiro and Washington, to mention only a few, are in the ascendant, while old European centers, such as Vienna, Weimar, etc., are declining. It is hardly necessary to emphasize again that this is not a shifting from Paris to Canada, but from Europe generally to all these new centers at the same time.

There is another colonial empire which followed toward its colonies a policy similar to that of the French: the Netherlands in their policy towards the East Indies. The Dutch also have fully acknowledged everyone as equal who accepted the status under the Dutch laws. They even encouraged intermarriage, especially in former times. Quite a number of men of mixed blood have attained high positions in the Hague, and nobody considers it extraordinary. "The fact of their origin is neither paraded nor concealed. Nothing is made of it." [26] It did not seem to be a unique statement when one of the leading officials declared, "Indonesian students in our universities are much more our equals than whole groups of our farmers and sailors." [27] This pre-

[25] Mencken, *The American Language*, p. 637. He points also to plenty of words deriving from French dialects but unknown to standard French.
[26] Nathaniel Peffer, *The White Man's Dilemma* (New York, 1927), p. 166.
[27] Snouck Hugronje, cited by Bousquet, p. 110.

vailing class sentiment enabled the Dutch Communist Party to have one Javanese elected.[28]   There were 32,000 persons in the Netherlands who were born in the Indies, the majority of them Eurasians, some pure natives, especially among the wives of returned Dutch. The ratio of these people to the genuine Dutch is almost exactly the same as the ratio of "Europeans" in the Indies to the natives. German racial fanatics talk, therefore, of the "counter-colonization" which through the racially unconscious Dutch endangers the white character of Europe.[29]   But, unlike the French, the Dutch have assimilated the natives legally rather than culturally. They have not cared to force the Dutch language on their colonies. Even among the people who were legally Europeans many spoke only Malayan.[30]   The second weakness of the Dutch rule has been the very small number of "Europeans" among more than sixty million Indonesians, perhaps about a quarter million.[31]

Because the Dutch did not dream of a future cultural unity, but respected the Indonesian civilization as a given fact, they could not envisage a unified body politic. They never expected that the naturalized Dutch finally would comprise the majority of all Dutch subjects. Since they realized that the time of outright colonial rule had passed, they developed gradually the idea of a kind of dualistic

[28] It may be noted also that an Indian communist was a member of Parliament in Westminster for some years.

[29] Steding, *Das Reich und die Krankheit der europäischen Kultur*, p. 272.

[30] Bousquet, p. 85.

[31] Among the 242,000 "Dutch" in the Netherlands Indies in 1930, there were about 42,000 genuine Dutch, 166,000 Eurasians, descendants from Europeans and natives, 9,000 Indonesians, 7,000 Japanese, some thousands of Chinese, Arabs, Portuguese, etc. (Amry Vandenbosch, *The Dutch East Indies*, Berkeley and Los Angeles, 1941, p. 7).

Kingdom of the Netherlands. Legally the Indies ceased to
be a colony in 1922. An increasing number of officials were
taken from the natives, beginning with the lower ranks.
The *Volksraad* came to be constituted of an equal number
of Indonesians and of all Europeans, Arabs, and Chinese
put together. At the same time industrialization started.
The *Volkscredietbank* has enabled the natives to accumu-
late capital and in recent years thus to finance industrial
enterprises themselves.

Under these circumstances the influence of the East
Indies upon the Netherlands increased rapidly, not so much
through the Indonesians living in the Netherlands, as
through the fact that the homeland often had to accommodate itself to the economic policy of the Indies, which was
directed from Batavia quite independently. Indonesians
regularly were members of the Netherlands' delegation to
the League of Nations and to the International Labor Conference. Emulating the British and using their terminology,
Queen Wilhelmina promised dominion status to the Dutch
East Indies after the war. The climax was reached when,
from the conquest of Holland in May 1940 until the fall of
Java in 1942, the real government was not the government
in exile in London but the government of the governor
general in Batavia. At that period it could be said that
"the leading current in the public opinion is the continu-
ance of the Netherlands and the East Indies as equal and
autonomous parts of a common empire." [32] The impact of
the Japanese conquest interrupted this development and
strengthened other tendencies, pointing to a renaissance of
the peculiar Indonesian brand of Hindu-Moslem civilization. It may contain more elements of Western civilization

[32] Quoted by Vandenbosch, p. 71.

than any other of these revitalized Oriental civilizations; apparently it will not develop into a new overseas center of Western civilization. The study of such trends will be rewarding even if they do not fully mature.

Despite all differences, Dutch colonial policy resembles the French more than the British. Even more striking is the similarity of the attitude towards the mother country of their respective co-nationals living in other political units. The estrangement in politics, in way of life, even in language habits between the former motherland and the Transvaal and Orange Boers has been similar to that between the Canadians and France. The dialect of the people in South Africa, the Afrikaans, is a written language today, and it is clearly distinct from standard Dutch. Moreover, the people prefer to be called Afrikander instead of Boer or Dutch. Britain, although not always loved, is becoming more important to South Africa the farther the common history with the Netherlands recedes into the past. Netherlands' experts who came into the Transvaal during its last period of independence were disliked as foreigners as much as any English would have been. The Union of South Africa is dominated by people of Dutch descent today. Johannesburg is one of the centers of the modern world.

In the French empire and the Dutch East Indies we have discussed two types of colonial empire where the trend toward shifting the center of balance has been checked by World War II and is unlikely to be resumed. The examples of Canada and South Africa, however, show that failure is due to outside forces, not motives lying in the character of the respective nations. We may, therefore, be cautious in referring the different outcome in the French empire to the strong position of Paris culturally and politically, in the

Dutch East Indies to the weakness of European influence. More important seems to be the fact that both powers have met the resistance of the renaissance of old civilizations. The power of Arab Islam worked from inside; the weak Indonesian civilization was joined by the aggression of Japan from outside. The result is the same.

CHAPTER VII

The Tragedy of Germany and
the Future of Europe

W E HAVE NOW DISCUSSED most of the European nations, purposely leaving the Germans and Italians
for separate treatment. They are the nations which represented the claim of European unqualified supremacy
in their present fight against an alliance of peoples led
by partly or completely non-European powers. Millions
of Germans and Italians live beyond the seas. Germany, deprived of her colonies, and Italy as the ruler
of a relatively unimportant colonial domain, may seem to
have been in the same position as many other smaller nations, though we have made it clear that the possession of
colonies is only incidental to our problem. But less powerful nations were forced to participate in the general evolution, willingly or not, consciously or not, while Germany
and Italy were strong enough, their military, political, and
economic power based completely on European resources,
to try to stem the tide.

Italy, not long ago, faced a situation not unlike the situation of many of her smaller neighbors. The influence of
the Italian centers in the United States, Argentina, and
Brazil was increasing, especially upon the illiterate masses
of Southern Italy. The national pride stirred up by the
Fascist revolution could not tolerate that. Mussolini tried

to bring back as many emigrants as possible to Italy and to
settle them in newly acquired colonies, where they could
be kept in close dependence upon the center of the Fascist
power. He dreamed of a strong Italy with a strictly centralized government which would be free from all overseas
influences. It was understood that even the largest empire
in North and East Africa and around the Mediterranean
should look to Rome as its center of political, economic,
and cultural influence. Nobody can say whether these
plans were possible at all, or whether they might have resulted in establishing a new Italian center in East Africa
overshadowing in due time Italy herself.

It is the tragedy of the German people that they did not
succeed in participating in the general European shift overseas. The bulk of emigrants left Germany before she was
united. These Hessians, Hanoverians, etc., left their countries behind in a mood similar to that of the Serbs, Ruma-
nians, Slovaks, etc., who left their home countries at a later
period. But the united Bismarckian empire after 1870 was
not ready to give up the emigrants as the small nations did.
The climax of the effort to retain them was only reached in
our time when the Nazi Party tried to reorganize all these
Auslandsdeutsche, Germans living outside the Reich. After
1870 the Germans of the Reich were even less prepared
to be influenced by the spirit, for instance, of the Pennsylvania Dutch. It is significant that the most obvious influence
was that exerted by some old emigrants of 'forty-eight
upon the Social-Democratic party while it was outlawed.
Economically, technically, etc., Germany of course was
influenced, like all other European countries, by the United
States, but not in any appreciable degree by German-
Americans.

Germany tried under Nazi domination to establish a centralized body politic comprising even foreign citizens of German descent. She tried to exert an absolute unquestioned power like that she had exerted over her former colonies from 1884 to 1914. It is difficult to form a fair judgment on this attempt at centrally directed colonial administration, because of the relatively short duration of the German colonial power. However, it is safe to say that Germany tried to govern from Europe, as France did, but without trying to assimilate the natives legally and culturally, as France did.

Although there was much talk about Germany's need to obtain colonies for settlement, at no time could a conspicuous number of settlers be sent to these colonies. That was precluded by climatic conditions and by the late period of acquisition. In this respect Italy's designs for Tunisia and Ethiopia were much more consistent, though unsuccessful.

The accusation of misgovernment in the former German colonies may be very much exaggerated; the mistake was in the wrong psychological approach. To the end even non-Nazi German authors defended, or tried to explain, German colonial methods by citing analogous procedures from the past of other colonial powers. Similarly the Nazis tried to defend their racial discrimination against the Jews by citing analogous Jewish behavior in the sixth century B.C. The behavior of the colonial officials may not always reflect the beautiful program of trusteeship proclaimed at home. But not only is it no longer possible to get along without proclaiming such a program, there is also an imperceptible transition from using nice phrases to gradually being forced to implement them. The English may have made grave psychological mistakes in their treatment of their colo-

nies, but, at least during the last hundred years, they
have felt themselves more or less trustees, who were
destined to educate primitive natives towards the perhaps
imperceptibly remote goal of self-government. The French
and the Dutch certainly have often misused their power;
but they have kept the door open to individual equality.
Moreover in all these nations there were groups and individuals who upheld the right of the natives to self-deter-
mination, and fought the doctrine of "the white man's
burden." The German conscience was much less troubled.
The Germans were convinced that they were doing more
than other peoples for the education of lower races, and
that these would enjoy well-being only if they would follow the lessons of their white masters. But they never
considered it possible that Negroes, Polynesians, etc., would
ever reach the same moral level as the whites. Besides,
Germany upheld a "materialistic" view of the colonies at a
time when this attitude was being strongly attacked and
changed in other countries. To look on colonies as valuable
property alone was the general attitude in former centuries
and decades, but in the twentieth century is an attitude
maintained only by individuals, no longer by whole governments. Thus Germany was the only European colonial
power in the twentieth century which attempted to swim
against the current, to counteract the general development
of that century, the shift from Europe overseas.

After the First World War many Germans realized that
Britain had yielded her predominance within the Anglo-
Saxon world to the United States. They realized it with a
malicious joy. They were inclined to see Britain the ultimate loser in the war; they considered Germany's defeat a
temporary setback only, because it left her central position

intact. Considering the world situation under the unchanged aspect of the central position of Europe in the
world, they assumed that Germany had only to recover
from the actual wounds to be able to pursue her old power
policy. These Germans did not realize that Great Britain
had yielded to a general trend, and that Germany as well as
all European nations should accommodate herself to the
shift of the centers of gravity. Instead, Germany entered
the present war with a completely wrong perspective. The
most decisive victories in Europe could not change the
general trend, because the new centers were not so seriously
involved.

It is somewhat surprising that the Germans themselves
did not realize the fact of this shift of centers. For Germany
has the tradition of shifting centers within a growing and
advancing national body. From the tenth century on, the
German centers have gradually shifted to the east and to the
north. It is the same movement which took place in Russia
and in Scandinavia, towards the virtually empty spaces in
the north.

Russia had to stop this movement toward Siberia for
some centuries, but resumed it in modern times. Germany
has tried to do the same, putting forward the theory of her
Lebensraum, living space. But Poland, Czechoslovakia,
etc., are not empty spaces, as Siberia and Lapland virtually
were. Thus Germany has been engaged in a twofold conflict, both with her eastern neighbors and with the general
trend of the century toward shifting the center overseas.
Germany tries to organize and subordinate all the Germans
throughout the world to the European center. There is no
thought of resignation, as in the case of the French Canadians, the South African Dutch, etc. There is no thought

either of tolerating influence from centers outside Europe. Whether or not the development to dictatorship is in the line of previous evolution, in respect to the natural shift of centers of balance Germany has tried to change the general trend of development. She seems to be the only important nation unfit to shift her center from Europe.

Whether the Germans have accepted new values brought to them by the victors, only the future can show. Maybe they will change these values completely. Some experts on German mentality asserted that even communism, if ruling in Germany, would be a "German communism," not the Russian one. Whatever the political development may be, Germans are forced to take cognizance of foreign ways of life. The direct and indirect influence of ideas born outside of Europe can no longer be avoided. The influence of the American individual soldier may not go further than to teach the use of chewing gum. The prisoners of war, even those carefully indoctrinated by the Russians, may be mistrusted. This is even more true of the few returning emigrant politicians, but added together such influences are significant. Before the war, Latin, French, and Greek ranked in German higher education at least on a par with English. They are yielding more and more to English, and Russian is coming along. Each language opens the way to foreign literature and foreign influence.

New centers of Western civilization are developing in America, South Africa, Australia, and Northern Asia. These centers have attained such a distinct existence that their future development seems secured, whatever the fate of Europe may be. But it will not be a matter of indifference for the particular shape of their future existence whether Europe recovers from the present crisis, whether

Europe will take a leading part in the future political, economic, and cultural development of the world. It is sufficient to hint at the heavy economic losses in war materials and unproductive operations, at the losses of spiritual capacities in all the able men who will die before their time, at the lower level of education allowed to growing youth, who will determine the intellectual capacity of at least one generation. It is sufficient to hint at the irreparable losses of lives, happiness, courage to face life, of cultural values — all destroyed together with the old towns in Europe. Although literally the whole world shares these losses, there is no doubt that the greatest havoc of this present war is being wrought in European areas. History reports that Central Europe recovered after the destruction of the Thirty Years' War, but the recovery took at least a century. Europe had not yet recovered from the First World War when the Second World War broke out. Moreover, mere recovery will not be sufficient to reëstablish Europe's leading position. Europe's development will have to outstrip again the development of those non-European centers, which during the last decades have developed faster than the old countries. We have tried to describe the dislocation of the old centers. Such a dislocation means a mortal crisis for the old center. It must change, or it will not survive. It can survive only if it can adapt itself to new conditions. In our opinion the two World Wars are but culminating climaxes in that crisis. We do not share the view of those authors, for example, who ascribe the economic ascendancy of the United States over Europe to the disaster of the First World War.[1] On the other hand, we

[1] C. Delisle Burns, in *Modern Civilization on Trial* (New York, 1931), p. 115, gives characteristic expression to this widespread idea: "The

ascribe the two World Wars to the disintegration of the old relations between Europe and the other continents through the economic ascendancy of the latter. We should also like to avoid a formula which implies that "America destroys the balance of the Old World." [2] Europe has not adjusted herself to the consequences of an evolution she herself started. Europe, therefore, must either transform herself or succumb as a cultural entity; but there is nothing which points to a return of the old supremacy of Europe as the only center of Western civilization. Germany might have restored the political supremacy for a while. It is almost unthinkable that she could have destroyed all the cultural centers outside of Europe. She almost destroyed most of the cultural centers in her neighborhood in Europe. She was bound to enhance by this destructive policy the importance of the remaining cultural centers overseas. Their relative importance will gain also through the fact that Germany has lowered her own cultural standard. The diversion of youth from mental training to pure military bodywork has taken place in all belligerent countries, but everywhere else it has occurred only since the outbreak of the war, and will not outlast it. The limitation of all higher studies began in Germany in 1933. It is bound definitely to lower Germany's cultural standard. It may appear that only defeat has wrought irreparable damage, that a victorous Germany could have caught up with these years of

---

motor car and the cinema would not have come from America to Europe, if it had not been for the Great War"; for Europe would otherwise have had time to develop the same industries herself! Even authors like Miller and Hill (*The Giant of the Western World*), who recognize the emergence of a new North Atlantic civilization, try to explain (p. 7) the strong American contribution to it by the mere accident that a European post-war depression coincided with an American post-war prosperity.

[2] Miller and Hill use this expression on p. 225 as the title of a chapter.

neglected cultural activity. But the very character of the German victory would have forced her to keep her youth in the unproductive occupations of policing and guarding her rule. All the conquering nations of the past, Romans as well as Arabs and Mongols, finally had to employ their whole strength in garrisoning and ruling the conquered territories; they were forced, therefore, to leave the spiritual and intellectual functions to the conquered — Greeks, Chinese, Byzantines, Persians, and Indians — who ultimately gave their civilization to the rulers. Germany never was strong enough to rule the world as she ruled Poland. Even in Europe she had to rely on allies and to grant them a certain degree of individual development. Ruling other continents was possible only with the help of overseas allies, who in their turn would have been able after some time to push to the forefront intellectually.

Other trends pointed in the same direction. German population policy made some headway in raising the German birthrate.[3] But the very emphasis on selective population politics would have nullified its ultimate goal. The destruction of life and reproductive capacity in countries such as Poland, Czechoslovakia, Ukraine, Greece could not have permitted a significant growth of the total European population and would in the end have impaired

[3] R. R. Kuczynski, *Living Space and Population Problems* (New York, 1939). In this short but highly interesting study Kuczynski, using official German sources, shows that fertility increased from 1933 to 1938. While in 1935, 100 newly born girls had the expectancy at the then prevailing fertility and mortality rates of becoming mothers of only 80 girls, who alone count for reproduction, in 1938 the rising birth rate had enlarged the expectancy to 110. But still, making the necessary deductions for death in childhood, girls remaining unmarried, etc., to every 100 mothers in 1938 were born only 94.5 prospective mothers. If we also take into account Austria and the Sudetenland, with their lower birth rate, the number is only 91.

Europe's basis for competition with other continents. Mussolini planned to bring home numerous Italians from overseas and Hitler did the same from Bessarabia, Bosnia, Dob-
rogea, etc. This policy had its definite limitations quite
aside from the desire of the dictators to maintain "gar-
risons" overseas.

This is not the place to discuss the reasons for the delayed
economic recovery of Europe after the Allied victory. But
it would be fallacious to assume that a German victory
would have offered better prospects. Germany herself
would have been spared the worst and conceivably even
been helped by reparations from the vanquished. But other
parts of Europe would have been laid waste. Even if it had
been to German interest to restore their economic capacity,
it would not have been to German interest to rebuild their
spiritual life.

Europe has been the great center of cultural life during
the last centuries, just because there were so many centers
of this life. The victory of Nazism, by destroying many of
the non-German cultural centers in Europe, would not so
much have strengthened the surviving German ones, as
it would have made more precarious European cultural
predominance by the necessary reliance upon the remaining
few. Of the many national cultural centers only the Jewish
one is destroyed in Europe beyond hope of recovery. The
Czech, Polish, Slovene, and Serb centers escaped by a hair's
breadth.

It is not necessary in this connection to describe the sad
state of affairs in which the German defeat left Europe and
the slow recovery which is going on. Prevalence of the non-
European powers will not be denied by anybody. But we
want to stress the fact that the fate of Europe would not

have been different in the case of a German victory. Its decline might have been delayed, might have been rather relative, but it was inevitable. The trend could not be changed, only accelerated by this war, less in the case of a German victory than by German defeat, but accelerated nevertheless. Also, a recovery will not change the essential fact. Europe can never regain the position it maintained during the last two centuries. The Age of Europe has passed.

CHAPTER VIII

Why Do Civilizations Pass?

THE AGE OF EUROPE has passed. History has recorded the passing of many civilizations. There is neither reason nor indication to assume that civilization should flourish longer in Europe than other civilizations lasted. But why is it that civilizations pass? Ancient civilization has attracted many scholars and many theories have been advanced from Gibbon to Seeck and Ferrero; only recently similar attention has been paid to the end of other civilizations. The idea that Western civilization might pass, too, would have been in the sphere of mere fantastic speculation only a few decades ago. When symptoms appeared that seemed to suggest such a fate, there was a division between those who envisaged such a prospect with alarm and despair, and those who saw in those symptoms only the pains of transition to a higher level. Some authors extended their investigation from research into the causes of the impasse of Western civilization to that of all civilizations. It has been suggested that Western civilization is draining its best blood in warfare.[1] Some authors are satisfied to state [2] that the end of all past civilizations has been accompanied by war. This is no explanation, but rather a description which explains nothing. Even when a strong

[1] E.g. Harry Elmer Barnes, *An Intellectual and Cultural History of the Western World* (New York, 1937), p. 1199.

[2] Frederick L. Schumann, *International Politics* (2nd edition, New York and London, 1937), p. 563.

foreign power has destroyed unexpectedly by the might of arms an older, higher civilization, we can almost always prove that the old civilization was already declining. This is true for the Incas as well as for the Mexicans; it is more than probable for the old Minoan civilization.[3]

But it does not even seem accurate that all civilizations have been destroyed by force. Some ceased to develop to such degree as is characteristic for periods of high civilization. Their tempo of development is no longer distinguishable from that of so-called static primitive societies. Toynbee calls this state petrified or fossilized.

A really flourishing civilization can not be destroyed by a conqueror. Its bearers may be defeated and subjugated, but the civilization itself will conquer the victorious barbarians. The *Greacia victa ferum victorem cepit et artes intulit Latio* . . . of Horace is true whenever similar conditions have prevailed. The history of the civilizing influence of the conquered Chinese upon the conquering Ch'in, Mongols, and Manchus is known. So it was in India, when Mongols or Afghans conquered the country. So it was in Persia, in the Byzantine provinces, when the Arabs overran their defenses. Internal disintegration is essential before external defeats become catastrophes.[4] Such internal disin-

---

[3] Arnold J. Toynbee in *A Study of History* (London, vol. 1–3, 1933, vol. 4–6, 1939) discussed the end of civilizations by external force and disproved this as the main reason in any case, but tried to show it to be a *coup de grace* to an already doomed society. *See* abridged version by D. C. Somervell (London and New York, 1947), pp. 260–272. For the little known Minoan civilization a convincing argument of the same process was made by Talbot F. Hamlin, in *Architecture through the Ages* (New York, 1940), p. 89.

[4] Unless there is an overwhelming discrepancy between the forces concerned. But the very conception of a high civilization implies that it influences a wide sphere and is not an isolated small community. The disappearance of the civilization of Easter Island may be very sad, but it

tegrations, however, seem unavoidable after two to four centuries of intensive cultural life.[5]

The historical fact that no civilization has as yet become older than a very few centuries is not sufficiently emphasized. The acme of Greek civilization is confined to the fifth and fourth centuries B.C., Hellenistic civilization to the third and second centuries B.C. Rome was certainly not a really cultured country before the first century B.C., and her creative period ended with the second century of the Christian era. We may reckon the Byzantine civilization at best from the sixth to the tenth century, the Arab civilization from the eighth to the twelfth. It is sometimes maintained that the oriental civilizations, especially the Egyptian and the Chinese, have lasted much longer; but if we take European civilization as a unit, from the Aegean civilization to the modern Western civilization, with spells of creative periods and depressions none of which lasted longer than three centuries, we shall obtain the same picture. The civilizations of the Old, the Middle, and the New Empire in Egypt are as strictly separated from each other by periods of disintegration, decline, rule of barbarians, and dark ages as those of Europe. And so are the periods of Chinese history, the periods of the Chou, Ch'in and Han, T'ang, and Ming. Furthermore, these periods are only from one to

---

is impossible to enumerate that civilization among the high civilizations of the globe.

[5] Pitirim A. Sorokin, in several works, most recently in *The Crisis of Our Age* (New York, 1941), attempts to prove this inevitability. His view is that the present crisis is deep-rooted, but that (p. 306) "it does not mean an end of Western culture, nor the perdition of Western civilization. It means the end of the fundamental phase, and a transition to another phase of the supersystem." This view is very close to ours, though the reasoning follows a different line. We differ from his point of view especially in regard to America.

three centuries long. The same is true of the periods of Indian high civilization and the periods of Mesopotamian civilization. The periods of high civilization are always short — a few centuries, sometimes hardly one century. If we take the whole period from the Renaissance in the fifteenth century until the present moment, the European period has lasted longer than any other period of high civilization previously. Perhaps it would be more correct to follow the suggestion of several authors and to separate the period of the Renaissance from that of modern Western civilization, the former originating in the Italy of the fourteenth century and ending with the religious wars in the sixteenth and seventeenth centuries; the latter starting with the Enlightenment in the late seventeenth century and closing — perhaps — in the twentieth. The center of the civilization of the Renaissance lay in Northern Italy; that of the latter in Western Europe.

At first sight the main difference between the Eastern civilizations and those of Europe seems to be that, of the series of "European" civilizations, each one arose in a different country from its predecessor: on the Aegean Islands, in Greece, around the Eastern Mediterranean in Hellenistic times, in Italy, again around the Eastern Mediterranean Sea in Byzantine times, a second time in Italy, and at last in Western and Central Europe.

But even this conception is deceptive from a restricted Western point of view. The Chinese civilizations had their respective centers in the valley of the Wei, on the middle Yangtze Kiang, at its lower estuary, and in the northern plain. Only seen from the West do all these remote locations seem to be in the same China. Similarly, the old Sumerian civilization near the estuaries of the Tigris and Euphrates was followed by the Akkadian civilization around Babylon. Assyrian civilization centered at the upper banks of the Tigris, and the Chaldaean period saw Babylon again as center. Even in Egypt the centers changed, although the territory concerned remained essentially the same.[6]

Why, indeed, have civilizations never flourished longer than a few centuries on the same soil? We reject the biological explanation which is sometimes brought forward. Biological youth, manhood, and old age are fairly good illustration; the expressions are well suited for description; but description should not be confounded with explanation. If we attempt to explain the fact that periods of high civilization have never lasted longer than one to four centuries we must distinguish between two sets of causes for their extinction. Most of these civilizations collapsed in a catastrophe which had its peculiar causes and is to be seen as a unique event. This can not be our concern now; it does not explain the apparent regularity of short periods of high civilizations. This regularity rather suggests that there are some inherent causes which are the same for all.[7]

Primitive and semi-civilized societies are characterized by traditionalism, stability, and conservatism. The customs of primitive tribes in Australia manifestly have been the same during many centuries. Periods of high civilization, on the

[6] A full enumeration of centers of civilizations flourishing in areas which had been colonial soil to earlier civilizations is given by Toynbee, abridged version, pp. 99–103.

[7] Cf. Sorokin. In accordance with his different approach, his explanation is much more detailed. His results are compatible with ours in general, though differing in some respects. His thesis of ideational, idealistic, and sensate types of civilization is of no concern for our thesis. Sorokin, however, on pp. 256–271, tries to prove it.

other hand, are periods of swift change. We should hesitate to call a highly developed society which is not, or no longer, producing novel cultural values, an example of high civilizations. Customarily only nations which produce new works of art and literature, better institutions, new ideas, are called highly civilized. Every new creation, each new material achievement changes established habits, evaluations, relationships. Diversities are multiplied and tensions result. Differentiation is a necessary concomitant of cultural achievement. But differentiation also is the source for alienation, dissent, distrust. In periods of high cultural growth not one but several new ideas were developed. The impulse of the Socratic-Platonic ideas did not result in a dominant school of thought, but branched out into several philosophical systems. As soon as the inhibitions of the archaic style were overcome, several different styles developed in Greece. The invention of the steam engine resulted in different technical developments. It is inevitable, however, that divergent philosophical schools should not only stimulate but also fight each other. Several contemporaneous styles enrich cultural life, as long as they have enough in common to please the same taste. If they differentiate too far, the adherents of one will try to stop the tasteless products of other styles of art. When man and animal power were replaced by use of water power, coal, and oil, the competition first stimulated search for more economic utilization, but now threatens to obstruct development of their full possibilities. Cultural advance means differentiation, therefore growing friction. Growing friction everywhere, in society as well as in machinery, means inefficiency at last. From this point of view we can understand why periods of high civilization come to a standstill after a relatively short time. It is not essential that wars mark final destruction, as Schumann states; perhaps in this respect Spengler saw more clearly, with his definition of the end period of any civilization as the period of the highly civilized mammoth cities, which though developing extensive division of labor are unable to create valuable innovations. He calls such civilized but uncreative populations the fellah-type of mankind. Alexandria in the later centuries of antiquity, Byzantium in the later medieval period, Peking under the later Manchus, may exemplify this type of passing civilization. Although possessing many attributes of high culture, their civilizations are comparable to those of peoples who lived before the great periods of almost imperceptibly slow cultural development.

More recently Kroeber expressed a similar idea.[7a] He maintains that a new civilization starts with evolving new patterns. When fully evolved they can be used indefinitely, but nothing essentially new can be created, else it becomes disruptive. When this state is attained, disintegration starts. The end of a special civilization has come.

But this disruption is not the only way the end of a civilization arrives. A new conservatism emerges, different from the conservatism of primitive societies. Many individuals experience this secondary conservatism in their private lives. They strive hard to achieve something. If they succeed they not always look for new goals but try to secure what they have achieved. Political parties if they accomplish their once revolutionary goals become intent on preserving the achievements of the revolution. This may be a passing phase in individual life. It may be a tem-

[7a] Alfred Louis Kroeber, *Configurations of Culture Growth* (Berkeley and Los Angeles, 1944), p. 764 and elsewhere.

porary pause in the life of a civilization. If it becomes the supreme goal, the new conservatism is about to stop the rapid tempo which signifies a high civilization.[7b] In my opinion it is a sure sign of a progressive civilization when a creative people is ready to consider any new achievement as only a transitory result. It seems very characteristic that the American manufacturer is always ready to scrap his machine for a more efficient one, no matter how short a time he has used the old one. In private life the typical American is always ready to move, to buy a new car, etc. The typical European is tied more or less by sentimental bonds to things which have served him or his fathers. He may point proudly to his twenty-five-year-old car, proud because he was a pioneer when he acquired it, no matter how outmoded the vehicle may now be. Among reasons for the relative decline of British industry was the clinging of factory owners to obsolete machinery and outmoded forms of organization which had served them well in their time. The extreme type of this conservatism is the European who tills his soil under circumstances which are clearly a waste of capital, because it is the soil, the house, etc., he has inherited, where he was born, etc. Undeniably these European methods once were the most advanced on the globe. The American farmer does not know such checks. Even today there lives on in him something of the restlessness of the pioneer, his longing for new opportunities. The typical European is proud also, when he has succeeded and improved his situation. He may try to reach a yet higher standard; but he is ready to consider the next or the second improvement the best level attainable. Even revolutionary parties in Europe, socialists as well as fascists,

[7b] Kroeber, p. 37, calls this "institutionalization."

recommend as their ideal the utopian society, where further changes must no longer occur.

These tensions between the rapidly occurring changes which are characteristic of a highly developed civilization on the one hand and the primitive conservatism of the less educated members of the society, together with the secondary conservatism longing for fixation of the new achievements, on the other, become dangerous for further development. If then specific forces arise, they are able to destroy a society disintegrating from inner causes. Aggression by a strong foreign enemy is only one of many causes, though a frequent one. All the causes discussed by the historians of the declining Roman Empire — birth control, intrusion of foreign unassimilable ideas such as Christianity was in ancient times, discontinuation of authority and law, increasing strength of the lower uneducated classes, inadequate administration, economic changes, high taxes — may be correct in this or that case, but only as the immediate cause of the catastrophe. They can act on a disintegrating society, that is, a society whose members have no longer a common goal. But it is also possible that the secondary conservatism, overvaluation of attained achievements, may become so strong that further progress is brought to a standstill.

History teaches us, however, that there is a way out for civilizations to avoid the final catastrophe. This way is their transplantation to new, to colonial soil, as shown in this book. There are some authors, e.g., Sorokin, who see only offshoots of the original European form in overseas Western civilization. These they mark as destined to die with it. However, we have shown on different occasions in this book, how the character of the non-European bearer of Western civilization has changed, how the Midwest farmer, the Siberian peasant, the Algerian colonist, have certain traits in common which are foreign to the European peasant. Not all types of people can and will emigrate. This eliminates a certain amount of friction. The problems of the frontier enforce further simplifications. Not all institutions of the homeland can be transferred. The colonist has to eliminate frictions in order to survive; certain branches of knowledge, certain types of art, etc., have to be neglected. This opens the way to new developments, to the evolution of new patterns. This does not mean that the colonist leaves the achievements of his old cultural environment completely behind. Harvard College was founded six years after Massachusetts Bay, and San Marco of Lima and Irkutsk University did not come far behind the pioneers either. But the colonist has to be selective because he can not succeed if he carries all the frictions of the old country with him. Thereby the road is open for a new type of society and civilization, indebted [7c] to an older one, but able to move ahead because most of the frictions in the homeland of this specific civilization are eliminated.

Some question may be possible as to whether in an individual case a new civilization deserves this name or is to be regarded as a renewal of the older one. The main problem is not touched by the question of the right classification.

We are inclined to regard Europe's great period as near its closing moment, although none of the examples given above offers a close parallel to the way in which it seems to be drawing to its end. Certainly there is no gradual exhaustion of creative powers so that a relapse into inactivity

[7c] "Affiliated," in Toynbee's terminology.

would seem unavoidable. There is no onslaught of barbarian peoples on a disintegrating society like that of the Germans upon the Roman Empire, that of the Mongols upon the China of the Ch'in and the Caliphate, that of the Hyksos upon the Middle Kingdom. It would even be hazardous to draw a close parallel between the upheaval of the depressed classes in bolshevism and fascism and the disappearance of the ruling classes in late antiquity before the rising tide of lower classes.

Nevertheless, there is at least one historical parallel which may help us see more clearly some traits of the development of which we are witnesses and in which we are co-actors; this parallel is Hellenism.

CHAPTER IX

From Greece to the Hellenistic World: From Europe to . . . . . . ?

I T IS AGREED that Greek civilization achieved its highest development in the age of Pericles, in the fifth century B.C. The Greeks had beaten off the Persians. Athens, Sparta, and Syracuse were the leading powers within the Mediterranean area. Persia and Carthage were pushed back to a secondary role. This predominant cultural and political position enabled the Greeks to overcome the geographic disadvantages of their poor, small country. Greek colonies were planted on all the shores of the Mediterranean Sea. Greek merchants, physicians, etc., went into foreign countries; Greek soldiers joined foreign armies. The emigration did not lessen the power of Greece herself; it rather augmented her cultural influence abroad.

Although all the important differences between the fifth century B.C. and the eighteenth and nineteenth centuries of the Christian era can not be stressed enough, the similarities can easily be recognized. Europe had beaten off the Turks as Greece had repulsed the Persians. Europe reached a high level of civilization; it forged ahead of the older civilizations of China and India. Greece forged ahead of the older civilizations of Babylonia and Egypt. Europe, like Greece, became overpopulated; both tried to solve their population problems by urbanization and colonization. Both became dependent on imports of foods from overseas. Although there are instances when such imports were exacted by political means, in general they were paid for by the surplus products of industrialization.

One or two centuries later, in the beginning of the third century B.C., as in the first decades of the twentieth century of our era, the situation had changed completely. The Greeks were still the dominant race, but their centers had shifted. Rhodes, Pergamum, Alexandria, and Antioch had either superseded the old centers like Athens, Corinth, or Delphi or were rivaling them, just as in our twentieth century London, Paris, and Rome are still cultural centers, but New York, Washington, Toronto, Sydney, etc., have become culturally and politically their equals and are still in the ascendant. Large empires like Egypt and Syria, dominated by a Greek ruling class, were the most important powers outside of Europe. Today the British Empire rules over a great many non-Europeans. In the South American countries Spaniards and Portuguese have assimilated the non-Europeans. These modern countries represent different types. But it is possible to find ancient analogies for most of these types, from the assimilated oriental countries to the purely Greek ones, where the Greeks had driven out the natives from the territories of many colonial cities as well as from some major areas, especially in Sicily. There did not exist any large country populated predominantly by Greeks which could be compared with the United States. This is important for the later fate of Hellenism, but it is non-essential for our purpose. We are in the midst of a struggle to find some federal form for the European nations. The British Empire has accomplished such a transformation only in the twentieth century; in ancient Greece the

Achaean and Aetolian leagues were the first general federal bodies politic. The older leagues had always been dominated by the leading city, and the smaller allies had been virtually dependent. Who will not remember older leagues like the Germanic Empire, dominated by the Hapsburgs and later on by Prussia?

In the twentieth just as in the third century the great powers are located outside of Europe. The only really great power controlling a part of continental Europe is Russia, just as Macedonia controlled a part of Greece. Macedonia ruled wide territories in the Balkan Peninsula which were formerly unexplored barbarian countries, in contrast with those well-known civilized countries ruled by Syria or Egypt. Macedonia herself was hardly considered a real Greek country by many contemporaries. There are the same controversies about the European character of Russia and the Greek character of Macedonia.[1] In both cases strength resulted from wide territories adjacent to the relatively small civilized areas; the colonization in vast contiguous but uncivilized territories is analogous; so are the struggle for harbors on the open ocean and the basic weakness owing to landlocked position.

There also is a striking similarity between the economic conditions in Greece in the third century and those in Europe in the twentieth century which are caused by colonization in foreign countries. This similarity is the more striking as there remain the basic differences between modern economy and an economy using slave labor and,

[1] "Philip showed the Thracian, as we say of a Russian that he shows the Tatar. The analogy of the Macedonians in Greece to the Russians in modern Europe is a favorite topic with historians." (J. P. Mahaffy, *Greek Life and Thought*, 2nd edition, London, 1896, p. 21.)

by this use of cheap labor, barring scientific rationalization. But neither modern Europe nor ancient Greece was able to produce enough food to nourish the population. Both countries had older industries which could flourish only when markets were steadily increasing. Both passed that stage, Greece at the beginning of the third century B.C., Europe in the first half of the twentieth century of the Christian era, when their emigrant sons founded industries in the new countries. The old centers of production were and are being upset by economic crises resulting from shrinking markets.[2] It is more than a mere coincidence that in this kind of economic crisis both ages tried to improve their situation by planned economy. It is owing to the particular conditions of Hellenism and of twentieth century development that in antiquity the most thoroughly planned economies are to be found in colonial territory, while at present they appear in the old countries. The Greeks found societies with planned economies in Egypt and elsewhere; modern colonists have had to develop an individualistic pioneering spirit in formerly underdeveloped countries. But in both cases socialistic-communistic experiments were first tried in the old countries. It is entirely natural that the centers of commerce and traffic should shift to the areas of economic and political power. Athens, Piraeus, Corinth, etc., remained busy harbors and financial centers, but Thessalonica, Ephesus, Rhodes, Antioch, Alexandria, Byzantium, etc., came to equal and outdo them. Perhaps before this present war the economic position of London, Antwerp, Hamburg, etc., still was stronger than that of most new

[2] M. Rostovtzeff, *Social and Economic History of the Hellenistic World* (Oxford, 1941), I, 104, and elsewhere, especially II, 615, 1026.

centers, and only New York had really surpassed them; but many others, such as Montreal, Shanghai, San Francisco, and Rio de Janeiro, are catching up.

We shall probably never know exactly the population of Greece in the third century B.C. It is clear enough that even demographically the center of gravity had left Greece proper. The population in Greece was diminishing swiftly, not only through emigration, but also through a decreasing number of children, the killing particularly of new-born girls, etc. The shift overseas created not one but several distinct centers of population in different parts of the Mediterranean world.

If our knowledge of antiquity ended with the beginning of the third century, it would be doubtful whether we could grasp the meaning of Hellenism as a distinct type of civilization though intimately related to Greek civilization. For Alexander's conquest marks no break in the cultural field. There is a gradual transition. The same is true of the civilization in all these Western countries outside Europe. The two World Wars are important signs in the crisis of transformation, not its cause. We have been careful to point again and again to features which prove the emergence or existence of new nations with distinct civilizations. It is not too early to proclaim the existence of this new civilization, which we might call "Westernism" as differing from eighteenth- and nineteenth-century Western civilization [3] in the same way that Hellenism differed from the preceding Hellenic, or Greek, civilization. We have little doubt that such a differentiation will necessarily be made by future

[3] Dean P. Lockwood in the *Journal of the History of Ideas*, IV, 63–64 (January 1943), in a discussion about a revaluation of the fifteenth-century Renaissance, speaks of the "ex-Modern Age, the now nameless age, the period of the fourteenth to nineteenth centuries."

historians. Likewise the differences between the newly emerging centers in the United States and Siberia, in South America and New Zealand, have their parallel in the wide variations of the Hellenistic civilization in Egypt and Athens, in Syria and the Bosporan Kingdom.[4]

Hellenistic civilization was different from classic Greek civilization in many respects. Greeks of the Age of Pericles were mainly confined in their views by the narrow borders of their tiny city states. Hellenistic civilization was a cosmopolitan civilization, with a broader outlook, an appreciation of the human being aside from his local affiliation. The old classic city had its official religion; worship was regulated by the state. Hellenism knew state religions also, but, outside of the worship of some kings, everyone was free to have his own private religion. Hellenism was further characterized by the orientalization of religious life, and by the gradual replacement of religion by philosophical schools in educated circles. In classic Greece the primitive life in small houses was luckily supplemented by an abundant public life; while the house of the Hellenistic man became a comfortable and well-furnished home, public life in the large states became a matter of concern for a few people — the majority came into the open only through big public entertainments. Public recreation is only one, industrialization another, sign that life especially in the big cities was becoming more and more standardized. Certainly standardization began in the old homeland in the "phalanx," as it began in Europe in the uniformly clad and drilled armies; it became symbolic in American mass production. Modern

[4] These differences are sometimes pictured as overshadowing the basic differences between Hellenism and Greek classic civilization. See Robert Cohen, *La Grèce et L'Hellénisation du Monde antique* (Paris, 1934).

general education has helped standardization. Education was never as common in antiquity as in modern times, but education in Hellenistic times became more general and reached a higher percentage of people, including the women. Indeed the importance of women in private as well as public life was greatly enhanced.

The number of writers of the fifth century B.C., the Age of Pericles, is rather small, even when we count not only those whose writings have been preserved but also those of whom we know nothing but their names. But in the Hellenistic period we know the names of at least 1100 authors, and this figure is certainly not all-inclusive. Judging from the few remains of their writings, we may say that they wrote for the great part in a journalistic way. The parallel to recent developments is obvious. In literature, novels and short stories were much more popular than stage-plays and lyrics, although representatives of all types were produced. The life in large countries — the uniformity over wide areas, the growth of a large urbanized population, and spreading literacy — is common to both ages, and produces similar tastes. As long as art was primarily used for the prestige either of the country or its rulers, sculpture and architecture were its most convenient expression. Pictures are better fitted for the intimacy of closed rooms. The development of a self-reliant, sufficiently wealthy, middle class is the setting for the evolution of painting. (Here it may be noted that painting did not become fashionable until the Hellenistic period, but was the leading branch of art in Western civilization from the beginning. Climatic conditions certainly favored this development. Even in the West, however, paintings were to be found only in churches and palaces up to the end of the eighteenth century. Re-

ligious services in Greece were performed primarily out-
doors, and thus favored sculptural symbols; Christian church
services are usually held indoors.) Even in science, some
developments characteristic of the Hellenistic period are
seen beginning during the European period of Western
civilization. Consider first the development from the philosopher and polyhistor to the specialist.[5] Western civilization in Europe produced men like Leibniz, Goethe, and the
French Encyclopedists, but there is no sign that such men
can arise at present. Present-day conditions have become
much more complicated by the spread of civilization, just
as the analogous spread of Hellenistic civilization over wide
areas made third-century life more complex than life in the
small Greek territories of the fifth century B.C. It is characteristic that most histories of science discuss all sciences
together up to the eighteenth and fourth centuries respectively, but deal with the different branches separately both
in the Hellenistic period and from the nineteenth century
on. On the other hand, the advanced urban life opened new
possibilities for collective scientific work.

Most but not all of the features just mentioned have
parallels in modern times. This review of Hellenistic civilization was primarily intended, however, to give an impression of the characteristic differences between classic Greek
and Hellenistic civilization. Though many similarities are
very striking, we do not want to draw too strict a parallel;

[5] The analogy in the field of science is perhaps the most debatable.
For example, Sir William Dampier, in *A History of Science* (New York
and Cambridge, revised and enlarged edition, 1942), p. 41, draws a close
parallel between the "change from the synthetic philosophies of Athens
to the analytic sciences of Archimedes and the early Alexandrians . . .
and the change from the Scholasticism of late medieval writers to the
modern science of Galileo and Newton."

some parallels may be casual. Of the three main factors which changed the classic Greek civilization to Hellenism only two are genuinely analogous to the factors in the modern change. One is the transplantation of a great part of the cultured people from a relatively narrow homeland to new, vast expanses. The other is the destruction of the original connections in family, city, and state and the assimilation of individuals from all corners of the Greek world in new communities, the ancient melting pots. The third factor is totally different in ancient and modern times: the Greeks emigrated mainly into old, cultivated, densely populated areas while the modern Europeans have emigrated into uncivilized, thinly settled territories, in Siberia as well as in Australia, in South Africa, and the most important parts of America.

This third factor constitutes such a fundamental difference that one should be rather surprised to see how many parallels there are than how few.

There is no doubt that Greece was strongly influenced by the new Hellenistic centers. At the moment which we choose, the most analogous to our present period, Greece was still striving energetically against this influence. She fought it especially on political grounds; she was still unconscious of the new spiritual influence of the Greeks from overseas and even of Hellenized non-Greeks. The cultural situation is symbolized by men like Zeno and Diogenes, by the beginning of the worship of oriental deities, by novels like Xenophon's *Cyropaedia*, which presents an oriental ruler as an ideal for Greeks, etc. The parallelism to the cultural situation in present-day Europe is striking. There were certainly relatively more non-Greeks in Greece, owing to slavery, than there are non-Europeans in Europe.

But their intellectual influence is as negligible as the intellectual influence of the Negro soldiers in the French army.

It would be easy to list all the more or less important diversities between Greece in the fifth century B.C. and Europe in the nineteenth century of the Christian era, between the Hellenistic world at the beginning of the third century B.C. and the modern world contemporaneous with the World Wars. There are some factors which helped to bring about the shift of centers in modern times which did not exist in antiquity. We have emphasized, for example, the important role which steamships, airplanes, and the telegraph have played in the shifting of centers of gravity in modern times. All these were unknown to antiquity and had only weak analogies in the improvements of roads and means of communication which took place. But these changes were essential for modern times only because of the large distances and the stormy seas included in the expanding world, compared with the small Greek areas and the peaceful Mediterranean Sea.

On the other hand, in antiquity there existed in the East large areas with high civilizations, practically unconnected and unknown to the Mediterranean World; there were also slavery, a time-lag in technical knowledge, a preponderance of primitive polytheistic religions, relatively small numbers of peoples, lack of all the sources of power such as steam and electricity, etc., etc. All these diversities did not change the process of shifting centers of civilization, of economy, or of political power.

The only real pertinent difference is that Greek colonization took place mainly in countries of old civilization. There are some writers [6] who let this fact appear rather irrelevant,

[6] For example, R. Cohen at different places.

while they contend that Hellenistic life was a development of old Greek life without much contribution on the part of the new environment. We have no analogy in modern times of an intimate co-existence of two civilizations which may blend at some future time. It is rather doubtful whether India will furnish an example of such a blend in the future. We consider, therefore, that the difference — whether or not colonization took place in a civilized country — may prove important for the future of Western civilization.

We have pointed so far to the analogies at two different periods. We must now compare the ways in which the change from one situation to the other took place in antiquity and in modern times.

Any comparison seems difficult at first sight. There exists no event analogous to Alexander's conquest of Asia, although the discoveries of Columbus and his contemporary explorers are sometimes compared with it. We follow Rostovtzeff, who declines to see more than superficial similarities.[7] Nevertheless, other events invite comparison, if we confine ourselves to those points which are essential for our problem of shifting of centers. The conquest of Alexander is often said to be the beginning of and the reason for the Hellenization of the Near and Middle East. This is not true. Alexander's conquest was only the immensely accelerated crisis of a process which had been going on for a long time. Greek colonies had already been founded centuries before; the fourth century B.C., prior to Alexander, saw an increasing influx of Greek mercenaries, merchants, and some scholars into the Persian Empire. The Persian army, as well as the army of revolting Egypt, had its Greek mercenaries as well as commanders. Persian and other oriental noble-

_____
[7] Rostovtzeff, I, 127.

men made use of the skill of Greek physicians. Greek pottery and Greek coins spread through the Persian Empire.
Perhaps without Macedonia's conquest Hellenization would
never have been so thorough. Nobody will deny the
revolutionary changes in the political sphere wrought by
Alexander's expedition. But this belongs to a different
category. We want to stress that Alexander nowhere
started a new, revolutionary cultural development; he only
accelerated immensely the slow but already existing trends.

Yet more than merely furthering the progress of Hellenization, Alexander's conquest had a truly revolutionary effect
in bringing about the rather sudden appearance of the new
centers to be considered. Formerly the direction of influence had been from Greece to the slowly spreading Hellenized world; after Alexander the Hellenistic powers became much more important centers, influencing the mother
country. Old colonies languishing in isolation, such as
Naucratis or the Ionian cities, became active again. At this
point we begin to perceive the resemblance to the modern
experience. In modern times colonies were founded, were
influenced from the European center, broke away, went
through a period of isolation, and sometimes rather suddenly became new active centers. Although the transformation in modern times came much more gradually, sudden
changes were wrought by the Spanish-American War and
the two World Wars. South America's emergence from
isolation, the transformation of the United States from a
debtor to a creditor country, the emergence of a first-class
American naval power, the industrialization of Siberia, and
some other instances mentioned in former chapters are sufficient evidence.

From another point of view, as regards the internal European situation, the World Wars may be compared with the Peloponnesian War and the wars of the fourth century B.C. The Peloponnesian War started as a struggle between competitors for the "hegemony," the prevailing position in Greece, for the rule over the colonial sphere. The ideological issues were extant from the beginning; but only during the war did the cleavage between poor and wealthy, between democratic and oligarchic powers become the main issue and dominate all succeeding conflicts as long as Greece remained independent. Yet the Peloponnesian War brought Sparta the rule over the islands and colonies only for a short time. Its direct results led to the breakdown of all the powers in the Greek homeland. Only a few years later the Greek colonies in Asia Minor came under Persian rule.

There is no doubt that the First World War also started as a struggle for markets, influence, etc., between competitors with a roughly similar background. The ideological differences between the democratic Western powers and the militaristic, authoritarian Central European powers would never have caused the conflict. The entry of the United States, led by Wilson's ideals, and the Bolshevist revolution changed the issue completely. World War II and the tensions between the Allies after its end are first of all conflicts between irreconcilable ideologies. Proofs of this are the fifth columns and Quislings in each democratic country and the grumbling masses in the totalitarian countries, Germany included. Compare the period when each conflict in Greece brought the expulsion of parts of its own population, when exiles from every city were to be found in each hostile army. But this remained essentially a characteristic of the cities in Greece proper. Will it remain confined to Europe proper?

About 250 B.C., there began a reaction on the part of non-Greek peoples. The Parthians founded an empire in Persia, in all its program hostile to Hellenistic civilization; the Maccabeans in Palestine followed, so did the Armenians, etc. Nevertheless, the renaissance in all these areas was brought into being under the impulse of Hellenistic civilization and always retained certain Hellenistic features. For instance, the best known of these native reactions, the Jewish renaissance, did not prevent Greek from becoming the mother tongue of many Jews, for whom even the Bible had to be translated. Jewish scholars were forced to define their attitude under the impact of these new strange Greek thoughts and the Greek way of life. We can follow their discussions, preserved in the Talmud, seeing them at first fighting against this strange world of ideas, but ultimately absorbing them. At the end of the Dark Ages, Jewish scholars brought Aristotle back to Europe.

Nobody can deny that the parallel to the Far Eastern, Indian, Arabian or Turkish renaissance is very close. It is true that some of these nations — Japan, Turkey, and some Arab countries — were never directly ruled by Europeans. But even for this fact there exist analogies in antiquity. The Carthaginians, the Campanians in Lower Italy, the Nabataean Arabs, were rather more Hellenized than the Bactrians, Bithynians, etc., who were actually ruled by Greeks or Macedonians for some time. As for the Carthaginians it is significant that Aristotle chose the constitution of Carthage as the only constitution of a non-Greek country to be discussed with Greek constitutions. Greek mercenaries and Greek merchants, Greek money and Greek pottery, had decisive influence on Carthage. Even Rome had a Hellenistic period which tinged the genuine Roman civilization very definitely. But the influence on Rome belongs to a late period, when Hellenistic civilization was passing and the political and economic center was shifting again, this time to Italy.

This parallel between an evolution in antiquity from the fifth to the third century B.C. and modern times should help us, first of all, to prove that such a shift of centers as we consider to be happening at present is not a mere ideological construction, but something that really took place in former times. The parallel has helped us review briefly for a second time the development as a whole, after we had reviewed one country after the other. Although we do not minimize the differences between the two periods, we feel entitled to consider the differences accidental as far as our topic is concerned. It is usual either to overdraw analogies in history or to spurn them completely, but a sound use can be made of them. The physician, who has seen the raging of a certain disease in different persons, becomes acquainted with it and knows how to fight it, although he knows that every new patient may show slightly different symptoms, varying with the variety of human nature.[8] We dare, therefore, to use our analogy for a careful restatement of our pessimistic prophecy of Europe's fate.

The social and economic evolution of Europe seems to have reached a point where dangerous crises are unavoidable. The economic character of European Western civilization is based on steadily increasing markets and new sources of raw materials. This process has created new economic centers outside of Europe. As long as these centers could be kept serving the European economy their

[8] Crane Brinton, "Napoleon and Hitler," *Foreign Affairs* (January 1942), uses this revealing example.

growth enhanced the growth of Europe's power. Gradually, however, they have become independent, rivals of the
old European centers.

Such was the situation when Europe became involved in
internal crises. One of the immediate causes was the rise of
nationalism in a continent where historical evolutions had
created very complicated situations relative to language,
historical traditions, and religious affiliations. Another serious cause was the widening gap between classes, some of
them formed under bygone conditions. Still another cause
was the economic rivalry between the imperialistic powers.
Everywhere older interests, existing since the times of early
Western civilization, clashed with new interests. We have
seen that the actual duration of high forms of civilization at
the same place has seldom exceeded three centuries. European civilization is older than that. But civilizations, because of their non-biological character, do not necessarily
die entirely; they are sometimes able to change into new
forms when transplanted to new countries.

The immediate causes for the breakdown of such old
civilizations may be very different in different cases. We
have enumerated above some of the more important causes
of the crisis of European Western civilization: rise of nationalism, class struggle, clashes between vested interests
and new forces. Among these new forces the rise of new
centers, the shift of centers of gravity to new continents, is
very important. In the complicated body of human communities such a shift means a dangerous, even a mortal crisis.
Such a dislocation can not be a mere transportation, it is an
inner transformation. The old centers have to adjust themselves to new conditions lest they die. In our opinion the
two World Wars are but culminating climaxes in the one

enormous crisis. Europe may transform herself as the result of this crisis, or she may succumb; nobody can tell which with absolute certainty at the present moment.

Whatever the result may be for Europe, it will not alter the basic facts. New types of Western civilization outside Europe — in America, in Australia, in Siberia, and in South Africa — are strong enough to stand without Europe. The old civilizations of Asia — in China, in Japan, in India, and in the Islamic world — are awake, stirred by the European onslaught, but quite apart from Western types of civilization. Among all these rival centers, Europe's quest for political or economic leadership is hopeless. So it is in the cultural field. In the cultural field, however, the rise of new centers need not spell decline for the old. The shift to new centers has transformed their cultural heritage. The survival of the old centers beside the new ones may enrich all of them. The Hellenistic period is called the age of the Alexandrines; nevertheless, Athens remained a center of scholarship and artisanship. Its cultural role lasted longer than Rome's civilization; it still was efficacious during part of the Byzantine epoch. Such may be the modest future of European cultural centers. But for the whole of European Western civilization this means but one thing: *In general, the Age of European Western Civilization is gone, but transformed Western civilization may survive in new centers outside Europe.*

Index

Abyssinia, 75, 180
Abyssinian war, 51
Achaean League, 202
Aegean civilization, 191
Aetolian League, 202
Afghanistan, 142–143, 190
Africa, 43, 64, 166
Afrikaans, 58n, 176
Afrikander party, 35
Afrikanders, 43, 176
Aglipay, Archbishop, 153
Ahmediya, 165
Akkadian civilization, 193
Albania, 51
Albany, N. Y., 145
Aldan region (Siberia), 129
Alexander the Great, 204, 210, 211
Alexandria, Egypt, 194–195, 203
Alexandrians, 216
Alfonso XIII, king of Spain, 18
Algeria, 167–169, 172n
Algerians, 169, 198
Allies, 24
America (continent), 22–23, 149, 184–185, 208
America (United States): architecture, 82, 118 f; civilization, 100, 115–116, 119; Civil War, 81–83, 89, 94; competition, 84; colonies, 47–48, 124; education, 103–104; exports, 81, 83–85; farmers, 41–42; films, 110–111; financial crisis, 88; foreign debts, 86, 211; historians, 104; history, 106–107; humor, 100; industry, 83–85, 195, 205;

influence upon Europe, 81–97, 103–107, 111–114, 119–120, 143, 149; inventions, 82–84; investments and loans, 85–87, 96, 211; literature and writers, 18, 99–100, 103; newspapers, 41, 93, 112–113; painters, 117–118; power, 92–93; protectorate over Britain, 32; public opinion, 92–93, 94–95; Revolution, 34, 47, 79, 106, 126, 145, 147; schools, 106; scientists and science, 102, 105–106; Senate, 91; techniques, 82, 84; tourists, 88; war with Spain, 16, 18, 96, 121, 196, 211
American scene, 117
Americans, 50–51, 57, 80, 90, 94–95, 99–100, 103, 108–109, 117–118, 124–125, 151, 167, 172, 194–195; English speaking, 42, 65–66, 79
Andean countries, 26
Andes, 6
Anglo-American practice, 90
Anglo-Saxon attitude toward colored people, 165
Anglo-Saxon civilization, 101, 115, 120
Anglo-Saxon tradition, 80, 95
Anglo-Saxon world, 32, 98–121
Antarctica, 102
Antioch (Syria), 201, 203
Antwerp, 203
Arab civilization, 191
Arabs, 57n, 163–164, 175, 177, 186, 190, 213; influence, 155

government, 36, 38–40, 42–43, 44–45, 46–48, 49–54, 56–57, 60, 162–163; history, 33; humor, 100; industry, 11, 73, 83, 196; influence, 15–16, 93; investments, 11, 75, 86; Labor Party, 51; navy, 40, 52; Parliament (*see* Westminster); policy, 15, 50–54; refugee children, 62–63; schools, 110; statesmen, 33, 51, 68, 95, 147; subjects, 54

British Columbia, 65n

British Commonwealth of Nations, 31–77, 162, 164

British Dominions, 31–32, 34–47, 48–56, 57–58, 60, 63–79, 84, 89, 91–92, 96, 98, 100–102, 107, 109, 120–121, 144, 147, 150, 164; influence upon Britain, 51–56, 57, 141

British Empire, 31–77, 79, 161, 201

British Isles, 8, 32, 34, 58, 75, 80, 107, 109, 154

British North America, 63n

Buenos Aires, 16, 19, 21, 76, 116

Buriats, 141–142

Burma, 164

Burma Road, 52

Byzantine civilization, 190–191, 192, 216

Byzantines, 186, 190

Byzantium, 194

Caldas, José de, 20

Caldwell, 103

California, 26

Caliphate, 199

Cambridge, England, 101

Campanians, 213

Canada, Dominion of, 34, 36–42, 45, 46, 49–51, 63–68, 71–77, 87, 109–110, 124, 147, 159, 173; Parliament, 37, 92

Canadians, 33, 57–58, 65, 107, 172–173

Cape Colony, 40, 43, 50, 64n

Cape Town, 38

Caribbean area, 16, 46, 96, 143

Carthage, 200, 213

Carthaginians, 213

Casey, R. S., Minister of the Near East, 53, 71

Caspian Sea, 125

Caucasus, 126–130, 133, 139–140, 147

Central America, 16, 21

Central Asia (*see* Russian Central Asia)

Central Europe, 88, 184, 192

Ceylon, 60n, 164

Chaco, 6

Chaldaean period, 193

Chamberlain, Austen, 51

Chamberlain, Joseph, 68

Chamberlain, Neville, 51

Chicago, Ill., 115

Chicago, World's Columbian Exposition, 82–83

Chile, 4–5, 7, 17, 87n

China, 21, 52, 151, 164, 192–193, 194, 199, 216

Chinese, 65, 109–110, 153, 153n, 175, 186, 190, 191–192; influence, 163

Chinese civilization, 190–191, 192–193, 200

Christian Science, 114

Christianity, 197

Churrigueresque, 28

Cochin China, 168n

Colombia, 4, 87n

Colorado, 89

Indonesians, 175–176
Ionia, 211
Iowa, 156
Iran (see Persia)
Ireland, 40, 47–49, 57, 93–94, 109n, 111, 150, 152, 158
Irish-Americans, 150–151
Irish Free State, 35, 42, 47–48, 150
Irish Minister to Washington, 37
Irishmen, 47–48, 79n, 94–95, 97, 123, 150–151
Irkutsk, 143, 156
Irving, Washington, 100, 101
Islam, 127, 136, 163, 164, 169, 216
Isolation, 15, 31, 96, 98, 143, 211
Italian colonial empire, 179
Italian influence, 15, 178
Italians, 7, 115, 123, 178
Italy, 86n, 87n, 116, 117, 178–179, 192, 213

Jackson, Andrew, 147
Jackson, Justice R., 92
Jakuts, 141
Jamaica, 46n, 161
James, William, 103
Jamestown, Va., 126
Japan, 50, 86n, 87n, 116n, 119, 152n, 164, 165, 213, 216; war with Russia, 127, 141
Japanese, 65, 174n
Japanese aggression, 40, 41, 52–53, 71, 177
Java, 175
Javanese, 174
Jews, 114, 115, 154–155, 169, 213
Johannesburg, 44

Kabyles, 168

Kaffirs, 50
Karachan, 139
Kazaks, 137n
Kazakstan, 128, 130n, 137n
Kentucky, 146
Kenya, 57, 163
Kharkov, 126
Kiev, 125
Kirghiz, 130n, 141, 147
Koran, 166, 169
Koussevitzky, Sergei, 116, 117
Kroeber, Alfred L., 196n
Kuibyshev, 125
Kusnetzk, 128–129

Lafayette, Marquis de, 92
Lamas, Carlos S., 19
Lancashire, 72–73, 81
Landsteiner, Karl, 115
Lapland, 182
Latin America, 3–30, 78, 86, 87n, 88, 98, 109, 118, 120–121, 138, 144, 160, 173
Latin-American architecture, 118
Latin-American influence upon Europe, 21, 89
Latin language, 183
Lourenço Marques, 51
League of Nations, 21, 45–46, 51–52, 92, 96, 175
Leibnitz, 207
Leipzig, 144
Lenin, 139–140
Leningrad, 143
Leo XIII, Pope, 154
Lima, 14, 16, 19, 197
Lisbon, 11, 159
Locarno, Conference and Treaty, 52
London, 25, 75–76, 88, 101, 161–162, 175, 201, 203